Spiritual Gold
Mayan Mysteries
For our Modern Age

By
Dr. Don Welsh

Dr. Don Welsh

DEDICATION
To LaVonne Rae Andrews/Welsh,
my beautiful raven-haired wife
and spiritual partner for life.

Copyright © 2015 Don Welsh
All rights reserved.
ISBN10-692366571
ISBN13-978-0692366578

ACKNOWLEDGMENTS

Thanks to Rev. Dr. Luis-Carlos Sanchez, a fellow traveler, and to the Ventura County Center for Spiritual Living, where their beautiful Mayan architectural design inspired and motivated my interest in the Mayas (plural form) and their spirituality.

I am grateful for consultation and/or proofing by Nancy Van Tassel-Caswell, Sapphire Grace, Jennifer Tombuelt, LaVonne Rae Andrews/Welsh, Susan Vasquez, Jim Peterson, Donna Brenneis, Wil Welsh, Anthea Rose, Jolene Ross, Claudia Sargeant, Jane Zeok and Rev. Patrick Harbula, author of *The Magic of the Soul*.

Finally, thanks to my daughter, Laura Kepner, for creating and presenting the Safety Harbor Writers' Conference and supporting me in being a part of it.

Dr. Don Welsh

AUTHOR'S INTRODUCTION

"Spiritual Gold" is a novel about a spiritual journey. Many of the characters are real with fictional names, the spiritual insights are based on the Truth as I understand it and many of the incidents and stories are actual events, though some I embellished. As you read, my intention is that you gain even greater insights about the Divine as you and I journey together.

CHAPTER ONE

"Gringo! Oye, Vaquero. !Move along! ¿Qué pasa?"

I cannot help but hear his loud bellowing voice as he shouts out commands.

His badge reads: *Sarjente Jorge Lopez*. Having attained the rank of sergeant, the airport guard has developed a manner of authority revealed in his harsh barking of orders. He nervously thumbs his rifle and I wonder why he doesn't use a hand gun instead of a rifle. I figure he wants to intimidate people, as if his scowling face and angry vocal expressions don't do the job.

I find myself perplexed as to why I am about to be victimized. The scene reminds me of something out of a

Dr. Don Welsh

World War II movie. Apparently, I am playing the role of prisoner being marched to a concentration camp.

My initial reaction is to yell back, to tell the short guard to "bug off!" giving him a fast punch in the nose. The only thing that holds me back is my ministerial title, and possibly, the rifle.

My parents had picked up the Spanish phrase, "¿Que pasa?" from Puerto Ricans when my Dad worked for a water works company in San Juan.

I was two years old when they moved back to the states. My brother and I forgot most of the language, except the phrase, *¿Qué pasa?* Our parents kept using it when they felt discipline was needed. And they said it harshly, much like the airport guard. *¿Qué pasa?* means literally, "what passes with you?" or "what's the matter with you?" It was negatively imbedded in my subconscious mind along with an idea that there was definitely something wrong with me.

That led to years of psychological and spiritual seeking to dispel that belief in the first fifty years of my life.

My name is Donovan Wales. I'm a mild mannered, peaceful person who has studied scripture, self-help books, and the ministry. I'm a former disc jockey. If you ask someone who knows me if I would ever yell at a security guard at an airport, they'd answer "Dr. Donovan? No way!" But the stark truth is that I have a distinct, biting impulse to grab that power hungry guard by his fat neck and shove his face in the burrito he holds in his other hand.

I say, under my breath, "Here I am searching for spiritual gold and what do I get? *Searched* by a pot-bellied, power hungry bird-brain."

How do I explain my angry reaction? Besides getting defensive about my childhood belief in having something wrong with me, I'm hungry. With only skimpy snacks served on the four-hour flight from Los Angeles, I guess I'm ready to attack anyone who gets between me and my dinner.

With my spiritual training, I have learned to block the expression of anger and negative emotions immediately after they have been triggered. It is simply a decision.

So, I remain focused on the business at hand, which is to get through the Mexico City Airport terminal calmly and without having customs, passport, or ticketing issues. Just the designation, "terminal" ignites an automatic fear reaction in me. "Is this the beginning of the end?"

Dr. Don Welsh

I also realize my large size may have intimidated Lopez. The straw cowboy hat I'm wearing makes me appear even bigger than six-foot-one. It must have triggered the short guard's defense mechanism, too.

Usually, years of spiritual introspection help me deal with outer world challenges. Even re-languaging from "problems" to "challenges" spontaneously transforms difficulties.

I have learned to live in the "now" and subsequently, I quickly move on, summoning a taxi for our party of three: my wife, Violet, and our best friend, Carlos. He had been one of my students, who advanced himself through the "ranks" of congregant, member of my Board of Trustees, Spiritual Practitioner, and finally, Assistant Minister for Reverend Violet and me.

Carlos understands my angst with the phrase, *¿Qué Pasa?* because I had told him the use my parents made of it. Having grown up in Colombia, he liked *¿Qué Pasa?* thinking of it more as, "What's up?"

"Over here!" Violet orders as she grabs my elbow and almost shoves me in the right direction. My size has never intimidated her. Even though she is only five-foot-three, she was raised to stand up to others beginning with her six sisters and brothers.

Violet wears her raven-colored hair long, pulled back at the nape of her neck. She is proud of her Native American heritage: Tlingit tribe (Raven clan) in southeastern Alaska. As a Hollywood actress, member of Actor's Equity and Screen Actor's Guild/AFTRA, she is multi-talented, serving as a singer, co-minister and author on her own merit and a newspaper columnist with me.

She has an attractive, slim waist, partially thanks to practicing yoga regularly. She interests people upon meeting them with her genuine, broad smile and sparkling personality. We married after my wife of more than forty years made her "transition," as we call death in our teaching. I think of Violet as my raven-haired beauty.

I open the back door of the cab and she and Carlos, who is only an inch shorter than I, jump into the cab, squeezing her between us. The cab driver asks us something with the word, *¿Donde?* in it, which I remember means "where." I say, "We want to go to the capitol of Yucatan, the city of Merida, and to the nicest Hotel in town, Hotel Yucatan."

Above the honking and airport noise, the driver evidently takes the nervous tone in my voice to mean he should speed along the two-lane road, swerving between cars, battered trucks, bicycles and pedestrians. His chuckle changes to a sinister cackle. I notice empty *Dos Equis* bottles under the seat and smell *cerveza* (beer) on his breath
and notice his full ashtray. The guy seems *loco*, (crazy).

He has long, menacing fingernails practically curling under themselves as he makes crude hand gestures at slower drivers, narrowly missing their cars as he frantically cuts from lane to lane.

My wife and I have just hosted a Halloween Haunted House back at our Spiritual Center. With a wry smile, Violet whispers, "male witch costume?"

"Checking his calendar on his phone, Carlos asks if it is it still *íde los Muertos*. The twinkle in his eye shows he caught Violet's joke.

He was reared in Bogotá, Colombia until the age of twelve. Then, his family moved to New York. He is well-versed in both cultures and taught me that *El Día de los Muertos*, the Day of the Dead, is the Latino way of celebrating the passing of the soul into the next realm of experience, or what some call heaven. I say, "I'm not ready to make my transition, yet."

Finally, the taxi screeches to a stop in front of Hotel Yucatan. What a relief. The circular drive has a shady park area with a huge old Banyan tree at its center. It's an inspirational entrance to Hotel Yucatan.

"This would be a great meditation garden," says Carlos.

"Let's check in and come back to these benches," I comment.

Even though it is located in the historic district of the modern cosmopolitan city of Merida, Hotel Yucatan still has a relaxing old world motif.

As I step out of the taxi, a warm wave of tropical air sweeps over me. It reminds me of the humid air I had experienced as a child, when my parents left Puerto Rico after a two-year stay. I feel a deep sense of well-being.

I remember that feeling now. My Dad had a sixteen-millimeter movie he had taken of his family. There was Mom with Adele, our nanny. We lived in a newer looking, single family home where I was playing in a sand box. The film showed my older brother, Wil, happy and carefree. I hardly recognize myself with curly blonde hair.

Dr. Don Welsh

Over the years, Dad showed that home movie many times, until I actually felt I remembered living there, even before turning two years old.

My reverie is broken with a sudden, "Your bags, Señor."

Maybe because I've been reviewing and remembering the adoration of my nanny, when I pay the taxi driver, I hand him a generous tip of U.S. "gold." His whole personality seems to be transformed. He gets back in the driver's seat and speeds off with a squeal of his tires. As usual, Violet visualizes Light surrounding him and continues her blessing of the car and driver as he leaves, looking for his next unwitting victim. Yet, the effect she has on the driver may change his dealings with the future fares. They might get treated more fairly.

I am uneasy. What is there within me that causes me to feel incomplete? Why do I still feel bothered? Is there really something wrong with me?

And, did I just imagine the tune of "Tijuana Taxi" reverberating in my head?

CHAPTER TWO

We walk through the wide, welcoming doors and into a floral scented lobby. "Welcome to Hotel Yucatan," says a smiling Señorita.

I feel there is an angel protecting us here in Mexico. It seems like an invisible, friendly spirit. I sense it will go with us on our anticipated explorations.

The Yucatan Peninsula is located in the eastern portion of Mexico. It is the place where the ancient people left signs of advanced knowledge and accomplishments.

I feel that to achieve all they did, their spiritual consciousness also must have been vast. That's why I had been inspired to take this trip. My first pulpit as a minister of a New Thought Church was the Center for Spiritual

Dr. Don Welsh

Living in Ventura, California. Its building is of a modified Maya architectural design.

"This is the hotel the architect stayed in," I say, enthusiastically.

"What was that guy's name again?" asks Carlos.

"William Stacy-Judd. He wanted to create a branch of architecture based exclusively on western hemisphere models, so he looked to the Aztecs and Mayas. As it turns out, the University of California at Santa Barbara teaches western hemisphere architecture today. Architectural students also study the church in Ventura and other buildings around L.A., like the amazing Aztec Hotel in Monrovia."

Carlos asks, "How did you learn about him?"

"He wrote a book called *Kabah*, which the Center has in their files. It includes photos of Stacy-Judd, smoking a pipe, carrying a pistol on his belt and wearing an 'Indiana Jones' type hat. It also shows some of the ruins he discovered, as well as buildings Stacy-Judd designed. The most fascinating aspect about the book is his frequent references to his 'Friendly Maya Spirit.'"

"Why'd he carry a pistol? Was it dangerous?" asks Violet.

"Apparently so. But the most danger Stacey-Judd encountered was getting lost in Loltun Cave, inhabited by an alleged thousand-year-old man. The Loltun Cave was on both itineraries as well as several Maya ruins which Stacy-Judd reached using a sharp machete and directions from his 'Friendly Maya Spirit'"

The desk clerk interrupts our discussion, makes a copy of our credit cards, and assigns two rooms for our overnight stay.

Our rooms are on the second floor. The bellman, who carries our luggage on a cart, points out the elevator. One look at it, and we decide to take the stairs.

"We'll meet you at the room." I say.

As we wait for the bellman to unload our luggage, I tell Carlos we'll meet him downstairs.. "Give us about fifteen minutes."

"See you in the garden," says Carlos.

"I wish I'd said a half hour," I whisper to Violet, my youthful looking, new bride. We had enjoyed seven years of marital bliss. I was eager to share what I knew of the Maya with her. We are both ordained ministers and co-ministers of a small, but dedicated group of spiritual seekers.

Dr. Don Welsh

The bell-hop places our luggage next to the bed. He is especially pleased to demonstrate the air-conditioning system to Violet. "You jus' lift the window like thee'se an'jou can adjus' it da way you like eet, Señora." As he lifts the window, a pleasant floral scent, *(is it plumeria?)* enters the room. It adds to our sense of peace and joy in this tropical atmosphere.

After unpacking our overnight needs, the two of us walk downstairs to the garden. Carlos had found a comfortable bench under the Banyan tree. "Join me and enjoy the tranquility."

Violet motions for me to sit beside her. She says, "Just meditate on the energy here and imagine the spiritual feelings of this place."

I make myself comfortable, close my eyes, and breathe deeply. I sink into a feeling of being so loved. I have a sense of immense well-being. Joy fills my entire body and I laugh aloud. Life is good and I feel so happy.

I am drifting. I'm lifted and realize I'm seeing soft clouds floating by. As I try to touch the clouds, they seem to fade in my hands. As I lose a sense of knowing where I am, the warm, humid air engulfs me. There's a gentle vibration. Birds are chirping. I'm aware of the splashing of water in a nearby fountain. I feel a euphoric sense of deep peace.

In my meditation, a wise man with a white beard appears before me. There's a hint of a smile on his face. I sense wisdom in the soft eyes of this being. I'm filled with a feeling of wonder. Suddenly, a bright light streams from above and I'm bathed in love and a peaceful emotion comes over me.. I'm overwhelmed by being so loved.

After about twenty minutes, I open my eyes and find that tears of joy have welled up and are spilling down my cheeks. I sit in the peaceful moment as I see Violet smiling. She puts her arm around my shoulders. We face each other and hug. Soon, Carlos joins us in a group hug. Carlos comments that he'd love to find someone with whom he could have a deep, spiritual relationship. I try to find words for how I feel, but none are needed. Violet and Carlos radiate feelings of bliss and self love.

We walk to the restaurant next door and the receptionist seats us at a small, round table. After ordering, our discussion turns to the adventures we anticipate for the next day.

"Hotel Yucatan was the first stop on Stacy-Judd's journey," I explain. "Our trip includes visiting some of the ruins he had to chop his way to, using his machete. We'll travel along the route Stacy-Judd wrote about, including 'El Castillo' (the Castle) at Chichen Itza, The Palace at Uxmal and the unique ruins at Tulum overlooking the Gulf of Mexico."

"I've read that those shores off Tulum are kind of dangerous," Carlos notes as our chicken enchiladas and spicy tamales arrive at the table, accompanied by the delicious smell of the Mexican food wafting from the kitchen. "There are thick reefs of coral where many a canoe was wrecked."

I take a bite of enchilada, then answer, "True, but the Mayas made a discovery of a scientific phenomenon at Tulum. If an incoming boat sees a small ray of firelight shining through an opening in the rock, the sailor knows he is lined up with a gateway in the coral reef that will allow safe entry. That knowledge protected the residents from unwanted invaders who didn't know the trick!"

"We'll have a guide, though, won't we?" asks Violet as she fills her mouth with a tasty bite of chili relleno.

"Yes. Baby, our travel agent arranged for local guides at each of the sites to show us the ruins. Besides, we'll have our Friendly Maya Spirits with us."

"Do we each get one?" Violet asks.

"I don't know. It seems like we'd each get to have a personal relationship with the guide. Just as we do with the Great Spirit, even though there's only one."

We talk until our stomachs are satisfied and the light has dimmed. We all agree to conclude the evening. I enjoy my last gulp of Mexican coffee, knowing nothing could keep me awake tonight.

"So, sleep peacefully," Carlos says. We hug and go to our "air-conditioned" rooms.

The Yucatan Peninsula boasts an ideal climate this time of year, with high temperatures in the eighties and nineties and a cool breeze at night with temperatures dipping to around seventy degrees Fahrenheit. After the stresses of traveling all day, we welcome sound sleep to begin our exciting journey.

We walk back to our rooms and are surprised that our luggage is in a different spot than when we left for dinner. Carlos continues down the hall, then calls back, "My luggage has been opened, too."

I look inside the largest bag. Some papers are disheveled, though apparently nothing is missing. Violet

Dr. Don Welsh

asks, "Somebody looking for that 'Spiritual Gold' you've been talking about?"

CHAPTER THREE

Despite the two-hour time change, I wake early. I use a mind-map to make notes of my dreams. In ministerial training I had learned several tools that helped empower me in many areas of life. For example, I learned speed reading techniques, memorization methods, journaling and mind-mapping.

From his book, *Using Both Sides of Your Brain,* Tony Buzan shows how mind-mapping can be used for taking notes, brain-storming, outlining, and making speeches. The technique uses colors, music, pictures and key words to make learning more enjoyable. I've used it to recall dreams ever since.

Dr. Don Welsh

This morning, I have a faint recollection about a thousand-year-old-man in a cave. I conclude that the dream is about my subconscious mind and the old man is my inner wisdom. So I place the words, "Dreams" in the center of a blank page of my journal and draw lines coming off of it. I use key words to symbolize my dream. I write "thousand-year-old-man" on one line and descriptive lines coming off the key word line. "White beard," "short", and "wise," are some of the words I use.

I then create an affirmation to incorporate the dream into my waking life: "*I am divinely guided in every moment by the infinite wisdom within me.*" I learned to write an affirmation for even disturbing dreams. For example, after dreaming I'm being chased by a lion, I affirm, "I am safe and protected by the power of Spirit within me."

Next, I adlib a Spiritual Mind Treatment, a five-step affirmative prayer. Ernest Holmes, the founder of the Centers for Spiritual Living, had taught this simple method of prayer over eight decades ago. It was the powerful use of this tool which led me into the ministry, since I have seen startling results or "demonstrations" and chose this teaching, philosophy and way-of-life as my ministerial path.

I begin by listing the characteristics and attributes of God or the Divine nature, claiming the particular qualities that would counteract the problem. So, I claim power and protection to align with Divine safety. This is called *Recognition*.

I then move into the second step of Treatment, *Unification*. The purpose of this step is to identify or unify with God or Spirit, realizing I am one with the Power for good. All of the characteristics and qualities of this Christ-like nature empower and uplift me to know and feel as if I *am* connected with God or the Divine.

Feeling the Presence of this Love Energy of the Universe, I claim the particular Good I desire. I state my highest intentions. This step is like an affirmation; a brief statement of what I am claiming. I speak in the present tense, avoiding any negative proclamations and knowing that I already possess what the Creator desires for me. This step is called *Realization*.

The fourth step is *Thanksgiving*. I have an immense feeling of gratitude and joy in knowing how good God is. I joyously accept the good I have been given.

It's at this point that I can turn it all over to Spirit. I let go of any further desire to control the process and *Release*. I have done my part and now the Law of Cause and Effect recreates what I have affirmed. There is no longer a need to co-create my good or manipulate God to bring it about. The outcome is now up to Father-Mother God.

Recognition, Unification, Realization, Thanksgiving and Release.

This morning, I sit in the room's one easy chair and plant my feet on the floor and my head held high to assure a free-flow of Divine Energy. I gently close my eyes to make sure I'm not distracted by any shifts in lights or movement in the room. I speak my Treatment aloud, claiming:

"I know that the Infinite Spirit and Power for Good is blessing my life in every way. This Divine Nature within me brings forth all of the power, wisdom, joy, love and abundance I could want or need.

"My true nature is the Christ, the Buddha, the Krishna consciousness.

"Through it, everything good that I choose to experience is providing the blessings of this day and enhancing our journey among the ancient ones on this trip. I know this for Violet, Carlos, myself and everyone we encounter."

My mind is still a little troubled by last night's luggage disturbance. So I add, "I am always protected and all that belongs to me is safe, right here and now.

"I joyfully give thanks for this and every day and for my Friendly Maya Spirit, as I release my word into the embracing mind of the Universe.

"The law of cause and effect does the rest. And so it is!"

I then meditate, connecting with Spirit and feeling the Presence of the One, until I hear Violet doing her yoga in the room.

After we dress for the day, we hear Carlos tapping on the door and join him downstairs for the complimentary breakfast – a Mexican feast. Violet is pleased with the array of vegetarian delights. Carlos offers a prayer of thanks as we bless the meal. It includes tropical fruits, pastries, bacon, huevos rancheros, avocados and tomatoes.

We talk about our plans for the day. "What's on the schedule?" Carlos asks. I can feel his excitement.

"Our van driver, Armando, will pick us up at noon. He'll show us the ruins at Uxmal, where there's a well-preserved and huge structure called The Pyramid of the

Magician which has an interesting legend I'll tell you about later.

"The pyramid is tall, well over 100 feet and has a lot of steps, so wear your hiking shoes. There's also a large building called The Governor's Palace with several rooms to explore. We'll have an early dinner there at *Pancho's,* the hotel restaurant, then we'll check into our rooms at the Mission hotel at Uxmal, which is the next stop as we follow Stacy-Judd's route."

We go to our rooms, then to the front desk and check out. The clerk hears us talking about Uxmal and clarifies its pronunciation. "It is *Oosh-mahl,"* he says. He also comments it can be very wet there, but that the forecast is for dry weather – plenty of sun for touring and a clear night with the moon lighting the isolated ancient ruins and surrounding jungles.

Armando arrives and with his strong and sizeable arms, places our luggage in the rear compartment. Armando is stocky and apparently enjoys an ample appetite. His mustache is a thin stripe.

We enjoy the spacious seating and safe feeling of Armando's van. Even so, I visualize light surrounding us, the van, and the road. Through using this power of imaging or visualization of surrounding someone or something with light, I feel a shift in energy that has a positive effect, blessing the person or situation. While no real light is sent, the feeling of the Presence of the Divine makes a difference in how I feel about the person or situation. Stable as Armando seems, we give one another a knowing look, reminding ourselves that the Universal Spirit is our ultimate protection.

Winding through the streets of Merida, we are soon on a straight paved two-lane highway following the signs to Uxmal, a few hours away. As we get closer, we stop at a taco shack for a snack. We notice the weather prediction was accurate as we enjoy the sunshine, beautiful greenery and a spectrum of colorful flowers in the jungle. It seems like a travel poster coming to life.

Before we realize it, Armando pulls into the *Mission Hotel,* today's destination. He parks closer to The Pyramid of the Magician and the other ruins. The gigantic mound of rocks and clay bricks give me second thoughts about climbing to the top. Carlos gets out his camera and Violet her iPod to make a record of our spectacular adventure.

We decide to explore The Governor's Palace first and all the surrounding buildings. I'd heard these are some of the best preserved ruins in the area. Some of the surrounding homes almost feel as if the Maya families are just out for the day and we'll want to vacate their homes before they get back. I could swear someone is following me through the door to the largest living area in the home.

"What was that?" I ask.

CHAPTER FOUR

Carlos casually replies, "Just a snake."

"A snake?" Violet repeats. "Will it bite?"

"No it's harmless," says Carlos, "I used to play with them when I was a kid in Bogotá."

"To the Maya, the snake has the same characteristics as a serpent and the serpent was sacred.

Even so, I'm happy to move on to the pyramid, away from the shade and shadows. The air is starting to cool a little. As we walk toward the pyramid, I remember that Uxmal means, "thrice built" as it sits on the same sight as two previous structures. I remember to tell them about The Pyramid of the Magician and one of its legends.

"It seems a small boy was born from an egg, hatched by an old woman or witch and grew to adulthood in one night. A similar legend tells of competition between the boy and the king. One of the challenges was to build a pyramid overnight. He did and won the town's kingship.

"There are other legends about how the Pyramid came to be. One is that a magician-god named *Itzamna* built it in one night."

Violet says, "I like the version that the boy built it one night to gain his leadership position."

With a smile, I explain that "The Pyramid is 131 feet tall and is the tallest building in Uxmal. It evidently symbolizes the power of the highest God."

Violet leads the way up one side of the pyramid and Carlos follows behind us. Throughout our trip, he discovered that Violet walks very fast and her speed is even more exaggerated on the hike. She has excellent balance possibly due to her early training in ballet. Even though her legs are short, they're so powerful that if she studied martial arts, they'd be deadly (*but beautiful*) weapons. With her excellent focus, she leaps from step to step, eyes on the goal, to the top of the pyramid.

"You guys are very slow," Violet contends, half teasing. "Mind if I go on ahead?"

"No. We'll meet you at the top," I reply.

Violet soon turns a corner and is out of sight. Later, she would tell us, "When I got within about fifteen feet from the top, I saw a man wearing a Hawaiian shirt.

"'You can make it,' he said, 'Just a few more feet.'"

I mutter, "How can…I…make...it…over…this…last… stretch…of…rocks?

"Hellooo up there!" I yell.

"Come on up!" she says. "Wait until you meet…" she looks back to the top of the Pyramid. "Oh, I expected to see the man with the aloha shirt. It's funny. He was just there. Oh, well."

As Carlos and I reach the top, we are breathing heavily, We rest, enjoying the panoramic view over the tops of the trees.

"I saw a Friendly Maya Spirit," confesses Violet.

"Really? I don't see anybody out here," I argue.

"Well, he was right on top here and he helped me by encouraging me."

"How was he dressed?" asks Carlos.

"He wore an aloha shirt."

"Sounds friendly," Carlos admits.

Just then, Violet looks down. "I can't believe it! Even here, people litter," she complains as she picks up a piece of paper trapped by a rock.

She hands it to me and I know the routine. She's regularly picking up the trash she finds along paths, trails, nearby neighborhoods and city streets. I tuck them in a pocket and empty it when I find a receptacle.

Before I put this paper away, I notice some printing on it. Someone with a calligrapher's hand has written, *If it rains tonight, I'll meet you in Loltun Cave after lunch tomorrow.*

Without further thought, I put the paper in my pocket. It isn't supposed to rain tonight, anyway. But who knows we're going to the Loltun Cave tomorrow?

We start down the Pyramid taking it a little slower. But my mind is racing. Loltun Cave had been mentioned in Stacy-Judd's book. Local legend rumored that a thousand-year-old man lived there. I thought that might be possible because there are numerous caves and sink holes (called *cenotēs*) under the rock surface of the whole Yucatan Peninsula. Some of those caves are under Mayan pyramids. And if there really is spiritual energy underneath pyramids, as many new-agers believe, it could be surmised that a person living there might experience exceptional health and longevity.

Toward the bottom of the Pyramid, I notice hunger is getting my attention saying, *"If you want to live even another day, you'll have to eat now!"*

First, we need to show our credit cards at the hotel's front desk where Armando has already given them our names and even seen to it that our luggage has been delivered to our rooms.

Now, we are headed to *Pancho's* for dinner.

While we enjoy the fresh catch of the day, we hear distant thunder. "I thought the forecast was for dry weather," Carlos comments.

"Anything can happen in a tropical climate this time of year," I say.

"Yeah, like back home. At certain times of the year, a sudden rain can surprise you."

By the time we finish our flan, we notice a major storm generating momentum. We prepare for bed back in our room and as soon as we are ready to climb in, a monumental crash of thunder sounds, immediately followed by a noisy downpour. Violet snuggles in close as she asks, "What do you call that?"

Dr. Don Welsh

"Uxmal. I call it an Uxmal"

Violet laughs. "From this moment on, whenever we encounter heavy rain anywhere, we'll call it an *Uxmal.*"

There is no fourth wall on the room. There is a door at one end, two walls on the sides and a whole open end where we can look out on the jungle and the surprise rainstorm as we cuddle in our cozy bed. There's something romantic about a tropical storm. I kiss her soft, receptive lips.

CHAPTER FIVE

The downpour stops in the night and the bright, tropical, morning sun invites us to begin another day's adventure.

After climbing the Pyramid yesterday, I notice that my muscles are asserting their frazzled existence. As I empty my pockets, I see the note we'd picked up at the top of the Pyramid. I puzzle at the seeming psychic prediction of rain. *If it rains tonight, I'll meet you in the cave after lunch tomorrow.*

A tempting, full breakfast buffet satisfies us with fresh fruits, eggs and an assortment of pastries and meats. As Violet and I join hands to bless the meal, Carlos walks into the hotel restaurant and joins us. I begin the prayer.

Dr. Don Welsh

I affirm; "The Creative Source has presented us with this appetizing and nutritious breakfast and I know Divine energy guides us throughout this day and blesses us with joyful and uplifting experiences. Spirit's wisdom leads and protects us and with so much gratitude, I accept and know that the Divine law reveals all that is good in this very moment. I am so grateful Spirit returns everything I give, including love. And so it is."

I squeeze Violet's hand and we all enjoy the meal.

During breakfast, I share the note. My logic would have normally ignored the message. How could anyone know it was going to rain? And how would they know we plan to go to the Loltun Cave today?

Leaving the café, as we walk through the lobby, I notice Armando chatting with some of the hotel personnel and ask if we could confer with him. I want to know about what time we would be at the Loltun Cave.

Armando says, "We have ruins at Kabah and at Sayil and Labna. Then we'll go to the Loltun Cave. They'll have barbequed lunch available for visitors."

"Anything for vegetarians?" Violet asks.

"Beans," is Armando's response.

Violet laughs.

We check out and load into Armando's van for the short ride. We park at Kabah.

"I want to show you a new discovery, here!" Armando announces.

"What?" I ask.

"The Witch," he answers. "It's a formation in the rocks that actually looks like a witch."

Maybe it's my imagination, but as I watch, the Witch seems to wink.

"Oh, look!" Violet exclaims. "On that platform; someone drew a circle. Or at least it looks like one."

"It's a symbol for a feminine goddess," Carlos explains. "The ancient people carved them."

A surge of energy melts over me and a feeling of empowerment lifts me. I suddenly realize this is the first of the insights the Maya would reveal to us.

Spiritual Insight Number One: *"God is neither masculine nor feminine, but both."*

The feeling carries over to the next ruins. Labna radiates a sense of a new adventure. This is one of the ruins that Stacy-Judd carved out of the jungle with his machete; it was his own personal discovery.

Dr. Don Welsh

Sayil reveals the Maya's advanced technology. I call it "aquaducting" as it is a clever method for transporting water via aqueducts. The Romans were known for transporting fresh water from lakes and streams downhill toward population centers. It doesn't take too much of a heightened elevation for the water to drain from a large canal into smaller ones and spread into various rooms for use. The Romans surely didn't have anything on the Mayas!

We arrive at the Loltun Cave at mid-day. The bulk of the lunch crowd has already paid their admission and entered a dining area. We proceed and find a table. The waiter invites us to help ourselves to the buffet. As a professional courtesy, Armando is not required to pay for the tour of the cave, but joins us for lunch. Carlos and I enjoy the barbequed pork sandwiches and Violet finds much more than beans: cheese, salad, fruit and rolls.

"The tour is going to begin in five minutes," Armando soon announces.

As we get up from the lunch table, I spot a piece of paper on the floor, about the size of the one Violet had found on the Pyramid at Uxmal. I bend down and pick it up. A guide notices me with the folded paper and warns me, "Señor, por favor, do not litter." I start to deny my involvement, but stop short as I really don't want to create a fuss.

Violet leads the way as the three of us join the line and the tour starts. A middle-aged man with a thick accent narrates:

"Bienvenidos to the Loltun Cave, one of the deepest natural caves in the region. Please stay in line and keep up with the rest of us."

Just as we lose sight of the light above the surface, we notice a thunderstorm and soon leave it behind.

A young woman guide brings up the end of the line and makes sure there are no stragglers.

Bare light bulbs are scattered about every ten feet as the cooler subterranean air washes over us. We walk down, down, down and farther down.

"How far beneath the surface do you think we are?" Carlos asks.

"I estimate we must be fifty-feet down," I say.

The guide points out thick stalactites projecting practically to the floor of the cave.

"I remember studying those in geology classes in college," I recall. "The ones coming down from the ceiling of the cave are stalactites. They reach down to form columns with the stalagmites, which seem to reach up to capture the *might* of lofty goals where they meet the stalactites."

I remembered a trick the professor had given us for telling them apart: "The ones on the ceilings have to hold on *tight*, so they are the stalactites," said the professor. And there is *might* in being grounded solidly to the floor, so the stalagmites are strong as they reach up." When the two meet, they become columns.

At one point, where there are long columns of various colors, the tour guide stops and strikes a column with his knuckle. It makes a melodic tone and echoes off nearby columns making an eerie sound.

Periodically, the bulbs flicker off and on. Violet says, "I hope the lights stay on."

In the next moment, we are engulfed in blackness. A spontaneous gasp sounds from the group and the guide advises everyone to stay calm, assuring us the lights would soon come back on.

The weird reverberation continues and the pitch lowers until it sounds like a male voice speaking some ancient language. It almost sounds like a low, guttural, "Doctor!"

It's as if someone or something is calling me, Dr. Donovan.

I remember when I first heard that ministers could receive honorary doctorates through long service to a Center, combined with volunteering in various areas for our organization, such as chairing conferences and leading committees, the Home Office may confer the designation "Doctor" on a minister.

After a second or two, it repeats: "Doktorrrr."

Is this my Friendly Maya Spirit?

Dr. Don Welsh

CHAPTER SIX

A half-hour passes before the lights come back on. We ascend to the entrance and step into bright daylight.

"Violet?" I ask, looking around.

"Violet?" Carlos joins in.

"She doesn't seem to be with the group," I say.

"She was right here with us before the lights went out," Carlos points out.

"Excuse me," I inquire of the young assistant guide, "Did you see my wife? Did she go by you?"

"No, I was standing at the edge of the group during the black-out. I would have felt anyone going past me."

I stand aside and let the line of people go by while waiting for the main guard. When he reaches me, I ask, "Señor, did you see my wife?"

"Is she the pretty, short brunette?"

"That's right."

"No. I don't think so," says the man. "Let's go up to the cave's entryway. Maybe she's there."

My heart is beating rapidly, as we follow the slow moving group. I try to squeeze by some of the folks. "Excuse me. Excuse me. Pardon me," I say. "I'm sorry." It takes what seems like twice as long to get to the entrance. But, no, Violet is not there.

I ask the guide about using the microphone to ask the crowd if anyone has seen Violet.

"Señor, do you speak Español?" he asks.

"No. Not really," I admit.

"I'll do it, then," says the guide. Immediately he asks if anyone has seen the pretty brunette American tourist. He speaks Spanish, so I'm not absolutely sure he has asked the right question.

No one responds. By now, I feel beyond concerned. I have a panicked sensation. My stomach is turning upside down. The rain has stopped, and as Armando pulls up in the van for us to continue our journey, I tell him about missing Violet and that we absolutely HAVE to find her NOW!

"What can we do?" I ask.

Armando goes to the manager of the cave tours and says, "The Americanos are very upset and we need to make every effort to find her."

The manager offers a plan, "We will organize a search party."

"There is no alternative," I tell Carlos, who is aware of my panic and deep-felt upset at her absence.

"Don't worry, Dr. Donovan. We'll find her," he soothes.

But no one has seen her. There is no response. There is no Violet. It is unbelievable.

The manager has arranged for the about twenty employees to go back down in the cave. Contrary to company policy, I ask and am allowed to join the group.

"We are looking for an attractive Americana. She is brunette with a long pony-tail," he announces. "If you see her or have any clues, tell me and we will investigate."

Dr. Don Welsh

I am right behind the manager as we begin our descent. We travel down and when we come to any branches, he sends a few of the searchers off and the rest of the us continue down.

When we reach the bottom, there are nearby restrooms. "Maybe she went into the ladies' room," I offer. A woman says she'll check, but comes back in two minutes, with no Violet. As we ascend, the smaller search groups from each branch return to the larger group with no results. We continue back to the top. The manager's face, with the "worry" lines on his forehead, explains to me, "We are making every effort."

I notice a disturbance at the front entrance. A woman with red hair and a blue dress is crying and saying, *"Mon Dieu – ou est mon petite chou chou?"*

The woman is speaking French. "Has anyone seen my precious little girl?"

Carlos speaks French and answers her, "What's wrong, Madam? Is there a problem?"

"*Oui*. My little girl is missing." She has a boy about twelve years old with her. "She was on the tour in the cave, and I didn't notice her missing until we got back on the bus that was going to continue our tour." The woman is crying uncontrollably.

Carlos consoles her and assures her, "Now, now," he says in French, "We'll find her. You'll see, everything will be alright."

"Thank you, señor. Thank you."

Looking at the boy, he says, "My name is Carlos."

The boy shakes hands with him saying, "My name is Anton. Could you help us, please?"

Carlos reassures the boy and his mother, "I'm sure we'll find the girl. We're missing someone, too."

I tell the woman, "I'm Dr. Don and my wife is also missing"

"I...I...I'm Sherry," says the panicked woman, and this is my son, Anton." They shake hands.

A new tour is about to begin. I ask them to watch for a woman by herself. Sherry affirms, "Anton and I are going to go with the last tour of the day, to find Yvette."

"Good idea," says Carlos. "Do you want to go, Dr. Donovan?"

I say, "I'll wait up here. They could show up at the entrance."

Dr. Don Welsh

Most of the staff had left for the day, so I sit by myself waiting for my wife. I am anxious.

Eventually, it is quiet. Then I begin to hear the group returning. Carlos is holding Anton's hand when they come back to the entrance area.

"I can't believe it." Sherry is shaking her head. "Where is my Yvette?"

"And what about Violet?" I ask.

Sherry shakes her head. As the group thins out, I ask the manager if it would be possible to spend the night here.

"I am sorry," he says. "That is against policy."

I call on the Spirit within to calm the rising anger I feel. "Is it also your policy to abandon lost tourists who may have been kidnapped, injured or even murdered?" He busies himself shuffling papers on his podium.

Finally, everyone leaves. But I stay. "We need to lock up, now," insists the manager.

"Maybe you don't have the authority to make policy," I begin, speaking as calmly as my racing heart will allow.

"I have all the authority I need and the policy…"

I interrupt, "No problem. No problem. I'll just call the *Miami Herald,* the *New York Times* and *USA Today.*"

"Señor, señor! Why would you do that? No harm has been done."

Surprisingly, I refrain from shouting at him, but say, calmly, "I think these international publications would be interested in a policy that would leave a woman and a child *locked up* all night."

"What?"

"Maybe injured, bleeding, without food, without water." My voice, which carries at any level, begins to rise.

"Señor," the manager says, whispering, "What is it you want?"

"My wife! And to find the little girl. So, I want a sleeping bag and a flashlight. And I will stay all night until I find them."

"No, no, no. There is no way we can…"

"So, you're refusing to assure the safety of tourists here?" I start to make a move to leave. "I'll make my calls."

"Wait, wait Señor!" he says, chasing after me. He grabs my arm and turns me toward him. "You don't understand. I cannot change the policy."

"Well, then…"

"But! But, here's what I can do."

"Yes?"

Dr. Don Welsh

"I will have my men, with flashlights, to search the cave, all night if we have to." His tone is pleading, now. "But I cannot let you stay in the cave."

"I see. So you will have your men search until they find her?"

"Si! Todo a la nocha, Señor! All the night!"

Should I believe him? I search his face, consider the earnestness in his eyes. "Will you do this?" I ask.

"My word," he promises. "We will find her."

I'm genuinely grateful. I can let go, at least a little, and leave it to this man and in the hands of Spirit. "Gracias," I tell him, grasping his hand warmly with both of mine.

"You won't call the *Herald*?" he asks.

"When you find my wife and the child, I will tell the papers what a fine manager you are."

He nods. I take a deep breath and leave.

"Are you okay?" Sherry asks.

"Yes, much better. They're going to search all night."

"Thank God!"

"We'll return in the morning as soon as they open," Carlos says.

CHAPTER SEVEN

We notice Armando's van is parked at the curb. He agrees to take us to The Cave Inn to spend the night.

We check into three rooms. I will share a room with Carlos and Armando has a single. Sherry and her son will take the third room. We find a small restaurant next door to the motel, and invite Armando and Sherry and Anton to dine with us.

After we're all seated, I offer a prayer: "I know there is one Divine Intelligence blessing our lives right now. Spirit knows exactly where Rev. Violet and Yvette are and brings them to us. I see the perfect return and they show up. I am so grateful for their safety and perfect joyful reunion with us. Furthermore, Yvette and Violet are right where God is. I know they are guided to find their way back to us. They are protected and Divine Wisdom leads them. Right here and now, we accept their return. Love protects and guards Violet and Yvette. They are here right now. And so it is."

When opening my eyes, I actually feel surprised that Violet and little Yvette aren't seated at the table and realize I believed my own treatment so much that it made it very real.

We had the *albóndigas* soup and homemade Mexican food.

I sleep restlessly. *I am in Loltun cave. There is a large room with an old, bearded being talking to me. He says, "Your beautiful lady brings love to your travels." He tells me that Sherry is an angel of Love and Peace. I sense Sherry is lying next to Carlos. "Carlos," she whispers, "I love you."* At that moment, I wake up. I lie there thinking of Violet. I'm worried. I try not to be. I remember my prayer and think of the joy I'll experience when she returns.

At the first light of day, I'm up and dressed and meditate on the joy of finding Violet until Carlos is ready to go. I share my dream with him. He admits he's attracted to Sherry. "How old do you think she is?" wonders Carlos.

"She seems to be thirty-four to thirty-six," I estimate. Carlos is approaching fifty. He says, "I wouldn't want to rob the cradle, as they say."

Sherry is waiting for us as we knock on her door. She's wearing the same blue dress.

Armando is sitting in the lobby, reading the paper. "Let's get over to the cave," I say.

Sherry says, "You really love her, don't you?"

"More than anyone or anything." I admit.

There's a lot of activity back at the cave. We catch the manager's attention as we enter the front area. He excitedly tells us, "There's been a cave in," he excitedly tells us. "It blocked one of the passages. It must have happened during the black out."

"Oh, my God! Is anyone under it?" asks Sherry.

"We don't know." the manager responds. "In fact, we are checking to see if that's where the missing people are."

"Let's go!" I say, We can help!"

"No, we have extra workers here digging as fast as they can."

Dr. Don Welsh

A young man hurries by, saying, "We broke through," in Spanish.

A moment later, Violet emerges, walking hand-in-hand with a little girl and rushes up to me. Violet and I hug and kiss. "I love you so much, Donovan," says Violet.

Sherry exclaims, "Yvette! I'm so happy you're okay! Where have you been?"

"Mommy!" shouts the girl. She runs up to Sherry's open arms.

Violet is saying, "I found the ladies' room and there was this sweet little girl there. She was scared when the lights went out, I took her hand, and we went out the back way. I intuitively followed my inner path and let Light guide us. But then, there was this sound and the cave rumbled to a close."

I give her another big hug as I say, "I'm so glad you're alright!" Tears have formed in my eyes.

Sherry introduces us saying, "Dr. Donovan and Carlos, this is Yvette. And Yvette, meet Dr. Donovan and Carlos."

"Thank you for helping me," says Yvette quietly as she hugs Violet.

"Oh, you're very welcome, Yvette. You kept me company, as well. We're buddies, now."

As we start to walk outside, Carlos asks, "Dr. Don, I was just remembering that you found a paper on the floor. What was it?"

"I almost forgot myself." I reach in my pocket.

"Hmm. It looks like another note like the one we found at Uxmal. Here, let me open it. It's the same handwriting. *The fire shines in the mid-afternoon as you enter Tulum.*"

Carlos wonders aloud, "Is that a secret clue?"

"We were going to visit Tulum, anyway," I remind him and Violet.

Violet is obviously happy for Sherry and Yvette. She asks, "Sherry, can you join us? Armando indicates his willingness to take the three new passengers "for only a little bit more….a peso or two."

Violet gives Armando an affectionate hug as we all pile in to the van.

Armando takes us to Xel Ha, (pronounced "shell-ha"), a beautiful swimming hole in a bay along the ocean shore.

Next to it, there's a rental shack, especially designed to provide swimsuits, goggles, masks and fins for people to snorkel in shallow water. The deepest area is four feet deep. A colorful rope divides the swimming area from the ocean. Hundreds of bright colored tropical fish surround the snorkelers. We change into our swimsuits and everyone, except Armando, eagerly splash into the water. Carlos takes Sherry's hand and they step into the swimming area together. Her children follow, Yvette a little hesitant as she wades in to deeper water.

Standing on the shore, I marvel at the blue water. Violet emerges from the dressing room wearing a multi-colored, one piece swimsuit and sandals with sparkling gems on top. She carefully removes the sandals before stepping into the water. I help her in and follow behind her. The temperature of the water must be around ninety degrees. After fifteen minutes in the tropical water, I motion to Carlos.

"Are those barracuda I see?"

"Yes. But they aren't dangerous," Carlos reassures me. "These waters are completely safe."

We submerge again and I find it enjoyable to swim in the tepid water. I feel like I am swimming in an aquarium. There are schools of brightly colored fish and swirling aqua-blue, shades of greens and yellows, golden flashes, and multi-colored jelly-fish, matching the bright colors of Violet's swim suit. I relax, enjoying the soothing water which eases the tension of the previous day.

I see a larger shape about fifteen feet away. Keeping my eyes on the object, I remind myself of Carlos' reassurance, mixed with nervous anxiety. *These waters are completely safe.*

Yes, but that really looks like a shark, It has the dorsal fin sticking up out of the water. The fishlike image is five feet long. Its teeth are bared. *My God! It's closing in!*

At the moment it seems about to strike, I proclaim almost out loud: *I am safe, protected and the light of Spirit surrounds me now!*

Suddenly, I hear that eerie sound again. A low rumble, raising in pitch, much like a Buddhist horn, the dung-chin. Startled, the shark swiftly turns around and heads out to sea. My heart is hammering as I come ashore.

All of us surface. "Did you see that?" I ask the others. With widened eyes, Carlos utters, "Geez! Yes! I saw the shark starting to attack you, but then it was like a miracle. I heard that sound and the shark took off!"

"I didn't see it until its tail flashed as it left," Violet says with a shaky voice! "My God. Are you divinely protected, or what, Donovan?"

I tell her that I had affirmed, "I am so grateful for my safety!"

Dr. Don Welsh

I say, "I think we'd better get over to Tulum and find out what's going on."

As Violet goes toward the ladies dressing room, she stops at the office and tells the manager about the shark.

"Oh, no. That's impossible. We never have any sharks in these waters," argues the manager.

When she tells me what he said, I comment, "Well, I guess as long as something is protecting me, I won't worry about any danger."

However, when I tell Armando what I had experienced, he says he will contact a friend of his at the coastal patrol, to make sure the waters are safe for others. He then turns his attention to the short drive to our next stop at Tulum.

It is one of the newer ruins, dating back around eight hundred years. It was built right on the coast and seemed to be a stronghold to protect the land from sea attacks.

At 3 p.m. in Tulum, we climb some narrow stairs to an overlook. *The fire shines in the mid-afternoon as you enter Tulum.* The message in the note makes more sense. The Maya ingenuity included a tower on the shoreline, overlooking the entrance to the bay, where boats could enter safely. It acts as a lighthouse where a beam of light from a bonfire creates the light through a hole in a rock. It was aligned for sailors to easily pass through a break in the dangerous coral reefs. As long as they could see the fire through the hole, they knew they were in alignment for entry into the bay.

We admire the structure and enjoy meditating in silence. Next to me, there is a hole descending into a hollow below. As I sit quietly, I hear that weird sound again. I even imagine I'm hearing some words.

"I am the thousand-year-old man of wisdom. If you discover your inner feminine energy, the insights you desire will be revealed to you. Go to the most female-dominated place at Chichen Itza for your answers."

Dr. Don Welsh

CHAPTER EIGHT

When I share my insights with Violet and Carlos, they both respond with enthusiasm, "Let's go! What are we waiting for? Let's find Armando."

We find him near the exit, next to his van. Surprised at our sense of urgency, Armando hastily gets us loaded and we are on the road to Chichen Itza in less than twenty minutes.

The trip itself takes a little less than two hours. When we go through the gate, a young woman tour guide knowledgeable in Chichen Itza's famous Maya ruins, points out the highest structure, *El Castillo*, the Castle. On the way to the ruins, we are greeted by a stone statue lying on his back, with his knees tilted up. The Mayas call him Chac Mool. The guide tells us "Chac Mool's chest was used to hold still-beating hearts in sacrificial ceremonies." Anton shudders.

The guide advises us to use caution on the stairs, explaining that the Maya had small feet and therefore the stairs are very narrow.

At the bottom of the monument, are images of serpent heads. We climb up well over a hundred feet, following the jagged edge which portrays the serpent's back.

Our guide explains, "When the spring and autumn equinoxes take place, the sun shines on the serpent, casting its shadow on the ground when viewed at a certain angle. The serpent represents the God of Movement and Motion, or *Hunab Ku*. The Maya believed that the Milky Way galaxy is an image of *Hunab Ku's* entire body."

"So *Hunab Ku* is another name for the God that runs the Universe," affirms Violet.

This is Mayan Insight Number Two: *"There is only one God of movement and motion."*

I say, "I know that it really doesn't matter what I call God. I believe It is one Force for good, everywhere present, all knowing, and all powerful."

Having climbed to the top of the pyramid, we can see for miles. I am taken with a sudden, overpowering sense of peace and awe. It reminds me of looking at the view from the top of a rock outcropping in Colorado. In my teenage years, I would climb the *beehive*, named for its similarity to bee habitats perched on mountainsides. From the top of the *beehive*, I could see the high mountains of the Continental Divide. Even though the distance was great, I felt close to God looking at the beautiful scene.

The *beehive* was on our hundred-acre property ten miles north of Blackhawk, Colorado, off highway 119. I delivered my first sermon at nearby Cap's Lodge.

We had two horses, Bill and Becky, which my mother and I rode for two miles each way on many Sunday mornings to Cap's Lodge.

During the rides, I felt a spiritual sense of oneness. I remember, when I was about eleven years old, sharing an insight with my Mom that I had experienced, lying on the ground in an alfalfa field, that I wanted to be as much like Jesus as possible. Another insight I shared with her was a realization that the Great Spirit was similar to the energy of a school pep rally.

Violet asks, "Where did you share these insights with you mother?"

"It was atop a *beehive* I tell her.

"Were you as high above the ground as we are now?" she asks.

"Yes. About this high."

We see a door to go inside the top of the pyramid. There are submerged rooms, where we sit on rocks and meditate. I feel a peaceful, quiet Presence and remember, in the silence, that I want to find the place with the most dominant feminine energy. I whisper to our guide about it and she answers in a hushed voice, "There is a complex that includes a large building the Spaniards had called, 'The Nunnery.'"

It was believed that only women could stay at The Nunnery, so I'm thinking that certainly this would be the most feminine place here. I stop meditating, stand, and almost hit my head on the low ceiling. I stoop and then climb a ladder out of the submerged room and back to the top of the Pyramid. I appreciate a three hundred-sixty degree view of the surrounding area and a sea of tree tops as far as my eyes can see.

I make my way back down the outside steps with Carlos, Violet and Sherry and her two children following me. Our guide has already gone back down. As we reach the bottom, I leave the others behind and cross the courtyard approaching The Nunnery. I pass through a low door and am engulfed in cool air in the shade. I sit on a bench and feel the feminine energy to which I've been guided. I notice my sense of intuition is heightened and an overwhelming feeling of compassion and love fills me.

Sensing movement in the shadows to my left, I try to see more clearly. It occurs to me that the thousand-year-old man has finally decided to appear. Amazingly, he begins to glow as he says, "Doctor Donovan, welcome to your feminine side."

I become acutely aware of the love, acceptance and peace emanating from this Wise One.

In the darkness, I can barely make out the flowery pattern of a Hawaiian shirt. I feel a need to communicate.

"What is your name?" I ask.

"Quark."

"Like the name of the subatomic particle?"

"Yes, because I live at the deepest level one can know."

"So deep it surpasses the speed of light?"

"Yes."

"Does that account for your longevity?"

"Yes, because my body ages over a longer period relative to time."

I know that in quantum theory, quarks are elementary particles and fundamental constituents of matter. Quarks combine to form composite particles called hadrons, the most stable of which are neutrons and protons. Quarks are never directly observed; therefore, much of what is known about quarks comes from observations of hadrons. Similarly, much of what I knew of a Spiritual Being, I could observe from Quark himself.

I ask, "Are you here to teach me?"

"Yes, whenever you want guidance, I will appear."

"Are you my Friendly Maya Spirit?"

"Let's see. I'm friendly, I think, and I'm half Maya. The other half is Toltec. And certainly my Spirit is within me."

I say, "I can sense your loving Spirit and you certainly seem friendly."

"Not everyone can see me. I will be invisible to others unless they lift themselves to an equal level of consciousness. Children can see me, as can evolved adults."

"What about Violet and Carlos?"

"See for yourself."

As if on cue, Violet, Carlos, Sherry and her children enter the dimly-lit room. Violet asks, "What's the light?"

Knowing she can see Quark's glow, I respond, "Violet, meet Quark. This is my wife, Reverend Violet."

Violet slightly bows and says, "I'm pleased to finally meet you, Quark. I've been feeling your presence around us for quite awhile."

"I know," says Quark.

"Who're you talking to?" Carlos asks?

"This is our wise friend, Quark. Carlos, do you see a glow over here?"

"Something. . ." says Carlos.

"It's the thousand-year-old man," I tell him. "Look with soft eyes and feel the energy in the room."

"I feel the love and clarity and the warmth. Yes. I see a glow, too. Oh, it's you! Hello, Quark!"

Quark responds, "Hello, Carlos. You are a dear friend to Dr. Donovan and Reverend Violet. It is my pleasure to call you friend, as well."

"Thank you, Quark. I am so blessed to be in your presence."

Sherry says, "Hello, Quark. These are my children, Yvette and Anton." Carlos smiles.

"I am very pleased to meet you," says Quark.

"We'd appreciate your guidance as we explore," I tell Quark. "Will you join us?"

"For this, I am here."

"Are there other Mayas as old as you, Quark?"

"Not that I know of. I think it helps that I am half Toltec. We are all related to the Aztecs and before that the Olmec people. We are grateful to call such advanced people our ancestors."

I comment, "I've noticed the similarity in architectural style."

Quark says, "There are many similarities in our beliefs and spiritual practices, also."

Carlos comments, "I've heard that the Toltec people were warlike."

"More precisely, our people are warriors. But we don't make war on others, but rather on ourselves. We fight for enlightenment. Your modern day Don Miguel Ruiz is a Toltec writer who learned from Carlos Casteneda. Casteneda was the author of the writings of *Conversations with Don Juan*, a Yaqui Indian, knowledgeable about peyote, psychotropic plants, and hallucinogens."

"Oh, that's right," I recall. "One of his best known books was *A Separate Reality*. Are you such a teacher that advises those psychotropic plants for shamanistic purposes?"

"Not really. I believe you can enter an alternate reality without the use of those chemical aids. You already meditate don't you?"

"Yeah, a lot" I say. "And I'll admit, sometimes I get kind of far out – sensing communication from the Great Spirit and seeing a bright Light when succeeding at feeling complete after doing affirmative prayer." I add, "No drugs needed."

"You are definitely ready, then."

I have no idea what he has in mind, but I am intrigued. "Good," I say, "Where to next?"

Dr. Don Welsh

While Quark claims to be a thousand years old, I think he actually looks more like a man of seventy. I think he'd look even younger if he shaved his beard. His hair, moustache, and full beard still have some dark brown strands. His features are dark: brown, knowing eyes and dark golden-brown skin. He wears khaki chinos and a tan-colored Hawaiian shirt which somewhat looks like deer skin. He tops it off with a short brimmed, grey cowboy hat. He is not tall, about the same height as Violet at five foot three. Quark is muscular and thin. Maybe that is the bonus for working out for a thousand years.

Quark says, "There are more sites to see at Chichen Itza. I was here when my people developed these buildings. So, come with me to what your archaeologists call The Observatory."

We follow Quark out of the Nunnery. Violet and I follow him. Sherry and Carlos join hands with her children not far behind.. Quark leads us to the nearby Observatory. The rock walls form a circle. An inner circle creates a path which leads to the center. We can see a slot in the domed ceiling revealing the sky.

Sherry asks, "What is that for?"

Quark says, "The ruins are closed after sundown or you would be able to see the North Star, Big Dipper, and various constellations of the Milky Way through that opening. Of course the Maya had their own names for them, but they knew more about astronomy than your scientists have even begun to learn."

"Did they have telescopes in those days?" Violet wonders.

"Yes, and we had also developed an advanced electromagnetic microscope. If the Conquistadors hadn't destroyed them, modern astronomy would be years ahead by now."

"So, you had electricity?" I ask.

"Even more advanced!" Quark replies, "But that's not what's so important for you to learn. It is much more valuable to understand the importance of giving back to the Creator. When Spirit provides a deer for you to eat, give thanks for the gift and give love and caring to God's earth. Thank the Great Spirit for the many gifts you receive. Be grateful for all your relations."

Carlos remarks, "We use sports to teach lessons about cooperation, and getting along with others."

Quark says, "We, too, have ball courts for such teaching."

Twelve-year-old Anton asks, "Where is the ball court?"

"Follow me."

We walk down The Observatory stairs to our left and find the ball court. It is a quadrangular, flat area surrounded by spectator seating around the field. Quark explains the object of the game is to get a ball through the middle of a donut-shaped goal, mounted on a wall of the playing field. As you can see, the hole itself is only about six inches in diameter.

Quark explains that the purpose of the game is not necessarily to win, but to play the best. "Many times the captain of the winning team would sacrifice his life if his team won! If they lost, they would live to play another day."

Anton teases his sister, "Yvette can be the captain."

"Thanks a lot," Yvette responds.

"It was a matter of life or death, but the winners would be the losers and the losers were the winners," I observe.

"That's right," says Quark,

"Maya Spiritual Insight Number Three: *Sometimes losing is winning; sometimes winning is losing."*

Quark continues to explain, "We do not necessarily need to have things come out the way we desire. There is a Higher Power, a Superior Intelligence that sees more and knows more than our limited point of observation can embrace."

"What about the religions of the world?" Carlos asks.

"And God and Christ and the Holy Spirit?" Sherry adds.

Quark says, "For these lessons, come with me to the *cenoté*."

Dr. Don Welsh

CHAPTER NINE

Quark sets off briskly down a gentle hill going about the length of an American football field. As we follow him, he says, "This part of the Yucatan Peninsula is dotted with circular holes that natural springs fill with pure, fresh water. Each hole is one hundred to three hundred feet across."

Standing on the edge of the deep hole, Anton asks, "Is that a cenoté?"

"That's right," Quark replies. "Each of the holes can be a hundred feet deep and at the bottom, divers have found treasures of gold, silver and ivory. They also discovered small, mostly decomposed, human bones.

"Were they used as burial places?" Carlos asks.

"Of a sort," Quark answers. "Archaeologists theorize they were designated as places of sacrifice to Hunab Ku, the God of Movement and Motion. But that is not quite right. You see, the Mayas held a strong understanding about the nature of life. They knew it was ongoing, that not only can people live more than a thousand years in one body, but that the soul can live in more than one body.

Sherry asks, "At the same time?"

Quark says, "No, one lifetime after the other. Some call it reincarnation. There is no death."

Maya Insight Number Four: *"Since we are one with God, we are immortal beings."*

"What about those skeletons at the bottom of the cenoté, then?" Violet asks.

"Some souls made the choice to come into bodies that weren't quite perfect. The Wise Ones, Spiritual leaders of the Mayas, knew that physically or mentally malformed souls, who chose those conditions for this life, would be assisted in returning to the spiritual dimension for a rebirth. They gave these souls the spiritual understanding, courage and wisdom to be released into a cenoté for an ultimate sacrifice."

"Which was?" Violet asks.

Quark explains, "They were ceremoniously given back to the One, accompanied by that which humans valued – gold, silver and ivory."

"Were these, then, little babies?"

"Yes, when a baby came into this life, they were welcomed with such treasures to symbolize how highly valued they were."

Violet is deeply touched with the love that was shown to welcome the babies into the spiritual world. Soft tears fill her eyes.

"That says a lot about the God of the Mayas," I comment. "They obviously believed in a God of Love."

"Absolutely," Quark affirms. "In fact, God or Creator, or the Force or Hunab Ku *is* Love."

We all readily agree. "It's what we're made of," Quark adds. "We are all made of the Love of God.

Maya Insight Number Five: *"All beings are made of Love."*

I comment, "That is a basic tenant of our belief at the Centers for Spiritual Living. And these first beliefs about God, our nature and the nature of Life being eternal, automatically establish more beliefs that logically must be true."

Quark asks, "If you are made of God, what can you do as a Spiritual being?" Of course, we have a feeling that Quark already knows the answer. We take turns listing the possibilities anyway We can:

- *Heal any sickness in ourselves and others,*
- *Co-create ideal conditions for humanity and the planet,*
- *Forgive those who seem evil or hateful,*
- *Accept all others, (especially, those different from ourselves) with unconditional love and caring,*
- *Empower everyone to live happily, in abundance and prosperity,*
- *Know profound peace – peace of mind, peace in our bodies, minds and souls,*
- *Live life eternally,*
- *Cooperate positively, seeing whatever our creative minds can imagine.*

Quark's eyes sparkle as a smile forms on his lips.

I say, "I combine all these qualities and conclude with:

"Maya Insight Number Six: *As a Spiritual being, you can use your Divine talents to transform all life"*

Violet comments that not everyone knows and remembers they are made of Love and have these Divine powers.

"That's when we get students asking, 'What about Hitler?'" says Carlos.

"That's what makes teaching spirituality interesting," I add. "No force, not even God, can dictate how a person must live. It's up to each one to wake up to our inner Truth. Some people simply misuse their power."

Violet adds, "Eventually, everyone will get it, I think."

When we walk back toward El Castillo, Sherry's son is looking intently above the castle. Anton looks up and sees a beam of light connecting the top of the pyramid with the sky above. "What the..."

I follow his gaze, and am amazed at the sight.

"Quark, what am I seeing?"

Quark says, "We must be having what they call a photon storm."

"Quite a sight," says Carlos.

"What's a photon storm?" Sherry asks.

"It is something we've been noticing more frequently lately. Photons are attracted to the pyramids and create spectacular views especially as the daylight dims, like now."

We stand in a circle and watch the streaming energy field surrounding El Castillo. Violet taps several pictures on her I-Pod device. "It's unbelievable."

We're all chatting as we return to the eight passenger van. We invite Quark to join us. Fortunately, there's just enough room for Sherry, Armando, Yvette, Carlos, Violet and me.

Armando drives us to Cancún, a little more than two hours away. As we travel, Quark points out that the Nunnery at Chichen Itza, Loltun Cave, and the cenoté were all allegorical, representing the subjective or subconscious mind. Just as the real growth activity of a plant happens beneath the surface, so also, when seeds are planted in the mind, the creative process births that which has grown in the subconscious. This is how creativity takes place.

Anton asks, "Is that how I was created?"

Everyone laughs.

Quark answers, "Clever fellow."

Maya Insight Number Seven: *"Humans recreate the process by which God creates the universe."*

"First, we receive an idea about what wants to be created. Then we contemplate, meditate, and imagine what is to be. Finally, we listen for ways that we can cooperate with the process. We create a plan and take action."

I add, "For me to ensure that the highest and best for all is being created, I receive ideas from God by *visioning*. In quiet meditation, I ask 'What is the highest idea in the mind of God about _____ (my life, relationship, marriage, health, education, children, job, events or activities)?'"

Sherry requests an example. "Can you give us a description of how *visioning* works?

"Sure," I say, "Right now, every one, let's close our eyes (except Armando, of course) and meditate on Spirit, God, or whatever you call the Power for Good."

I let a few moments pass. The entire van is still. Then, I remind them to just allow the highest idea in the mind of God for their lives to flow into their consciousness.

"It's like when Rev. Violet found me in the dark cave," says eight-year-old Yvette.

"That's right, sweetie," acknowledges Rev. Violet.

"I like visioning," Yvette says.

Sherry says, "That's a very grown-up idea."

I continue, "You can ask for guidance about anything at all in your life. If you follow what you receive, you'll always be on the right path."

Maya Insight Number Eight: *"For God's vision regarding an area of your life, vision for ideas about the highest good."*

Each of us has special memories and insights from today's experiences. Carlos comments on the photon show. Violet talks about helping Yvette. Yvette mentions the clear water of the cenoté. Anton announces he's God's creation, and I revel in the miracles of happenstance that have brought us all together. Quark just smiles in satisfaction.

It's getting dark when we arrive at one of the large hotels on the beach in Cancún. We wave "goodbye" to Armando, who travels home to Merida for the next few days.

We check in, Sherry gets a large room with enough room for roll-in cots for Yvette and Anton. Violet and I have a small room on the second floor overlooking the ocean, and Carlos is right next door sharing a room with

Quark. With our windows open, we can hear the gentle waves of the ocean.

The next day is replete with shopping for Violet and Sherry at the market in the middle of town and swimming and relaxation for the rest of us on the hotel's extensive beach. I remember a photo of me with my brother playing on a beach in Florida when I was two years old. My dad had joined the Navy during the Second World War and went to Officers' Training School in Boca Raton. The picture shows me laughing and the feeling of well-being burbles up. Suddenly, my thoughts jump back to the present.

The water is balmy as I walk along the shore barefoot, feeling the sand squish between my toes. I consider the warm water to be a baptismal immersion into spiritual love.

I start to trot. I'm feeling light-spirited, like the two-year-old again. The children, Carlos and even Quark all begin to run too, racing along the white beach. The children quickly out-distance us and we stop, bend over and laugh uproariously. Quark says, "It's good to breathe deeply into your lungs. You stay young that way. Your body is meant to be fully lived in, it is not going to wear out; it replaces every cell at least every seven years."

Dr. Don Welsh

I feel like a boy, enjoying the light energy, and letting myself play. The Divine qualities of Life, Joy, Energy and Love fill my being.

CHAPTER TEN

That night, I fall into a deep, fulfilling sleep.

The next morning, we all meet for breakfast at our hotel's complimentary buffet, which displays a myriad of fresh citrus fruits and local fare. We plan our next adventure.

Carlos relates that an old-time local man had told him about the beach. He related that it isn't sand, but cool, coral particles which feel soft and luxurious. We play most of the day.

That evening, we dine at one of the fine food restaurants. One tradition, that seemed irritating to me at first, is having to ask for the bill at the end of the meal. I learned that they consider it rude to present the check without a request as it might appear that they are asking the customer to leave. Now, I have respect for this polite custom. Interesting how our ideas can change when we understand the reasons behind procedures.

When we return to our hotel, we hear about a dance contest and Violet thinks it would be fun to enter. I'm really not a great dancer, but she is very good at any kind of dancing. Even so, I participate fully, acting as if I know what I'm doing. Releasing any concern about what others think, I feel guided and empowered by Violet's skillful leadership on the dance floor. The prize is a lobster dinner, which motivates Violet to excel even more. Not surprisingly, we win the contest and anticipate a delectable lobster dinner a few days later at the hotel's fine dining restaurant. We plan to celebrate our five year anniversary.

We awaken the next morning to another bright, sunny day. In addition to our morning spiritual routine, Carlos, Sherry and her family join Violet and me in the pool where a beautiful breakfast is being served at the swim-up bar. Fresh eggs and crisp bacon or browned chunks of soy are accompanied with fresh tropical fruit served with dark toasted bread.

We fill the next two days with beach play, bargain hunting, and enjoying botanical gardens in this tropical paradise. I notice that Carlos and Sherry are forming a contented connection.

On the third day, Armando returns to the hotel. We are happy to see him as he pulls the van under the portico. Armando hugs the children and they help by handing him their luggage. We all pile in and travel to nearby Cozumel via a long bridge.

There is a large cruise ship anchored off the coast of the island.

Cozumel is an oval shaped island offering excellent snorkeling, boating and more Mayan ruins to explore. The ruins are really just piles of rocks, which remind me of some old native ruins on the Tahitian Islands, specifically, on the island of Moorea. Violet and I discovered them on a mountain trail off Cook's Bay. We had made it a point to conduct a spiritual ceremony on the flat top of the largest ruin, blessing all who once inhabited it.

There was a possible nearby burial site which also received our blessing.

Violet seems to have a natural instinct to find such places. When we had visited relatives in the Seattle area a couple of years after our honeymoon, she found a cemetery where her grandmother was buried. She had fond memories of her grandmother's farm in Bothell, Washington, which was named after a relative of mine. The name seemed like a coincidence, until I realized that my second cousin, David Bothell, had settled there, having moved from Pennsylvania in 1885. The town was named after him in 1888.

It was late at night when we found the cemetery and peeked through the iron gate at the entrance to the graveyard. When Violet had pushed on the gate, it had squeaked open. Our shadows cast eerie images on the tombstones, especially after we had shone her keychain flashlight around the burial grounds. We joked, whispering that we must have looked like grave robbers.

"What was your grandmother's name?" I had asked.

"Violet. Violet Bollman," responded our Violet.

"I didn't know you were named after your grandmother," I said. It was the first I had heard of that.

Finally, we spotted a flat marker reading, *Violet Bollman*, attesting to the fact that her family's path had intersected mine.

Violet had thought aloud, "I wonder how those coincidences happen?"

"I call it *energy synchronization*," I said. "The energy field of one person tends to seek like energy-fields in another. There's a constant magnetic pull." Indeed, Violet and I could count at least four other times during our individual lives when "coincidental" meetings occurred prior to our eventual marriage.

Love reveals itself in many ways. When World War II ended, and my Dad finally came home after his stint in the navy, it seemed like an eternity to a young boy. He had brought with him evidence of his love for his two sons.
He had carved two toy boats that resembled the battleship on which he had served. There were even little nails connecting a thin wire to depict the railing around the deck.

When I think of his gifts to us, it gives me fond feelings as I realize how much time he must have spent thinking of his boys while he carved those boats. Although his manner was reserved, (typical, I'm told, of an engineer's behavior) I am convinced he loved us deeply.

I realize my mind had taken a trip into the past when Armando announced we had arrived at our destination; a beautiful, blue-green bay on the inside, western side of

Cozumel, so we can scuba dive. It's much like Xel Ha, but we don't encounter any sharks. There are more of those dazzling schools of fish.

We are pleasantly surprised when Armando returns and invites us to have dinner with him and his family at his home in suburban Merida. When we arrive, his wife, Miriam, welcomes us into her cozy living room in the adobe structure. Their home is filled with loving feelings. Their two children join us before dinner. Anton and Yvette are delighted to have playmates and before dinner, they go outside and play hide and seek, a universally known, cross-cultural game. "Who taught all kids to know this game?" I wonder.

During the meal, the children are so well-behaved that we can't help but comment. My own behavior showed some leftover childhood characteristics, of which I'm never proud. At the end of the meal, Miriam entered the dining room with a delicious looking flan, a whole pie shaped dessert, browned perfectly with whipped cream on the side. While cutting a piece for Violet and me, the knife slipped and while trying to catch it, I inadvertently dropped my piece on the tile floor. It landed upside down, the sticky juice soaking up the dirt. I reached for it, but Violet made a funny "don't do it" sound.

Carlos added, "No three second rule here!" I laughed nervously thinking to myself, "qué pasa con tu!." I mentally went to *What's the matter with you?*

I replied, "*Nothing! There's nothing wrong with you, Donovan! You simply were trying to do too much.* To compensate for thinking there was something wrong with me, I usually over did it.. My automatic response was to attempt the impossible. *I'll prove to everyone that I'm more than just okay; I'm a super-human!"* That's when my subconscious belief would take over and cause an accident.

When I was sixteen, my aunt and uncle came to visit us at the mountain ranch in Colorado. I tried high jumping over a porch railing, my hand slipped and I dove head first into the ground, six feet below. I broke the shoulder bone and dislocated my arm. The pain had been excruciating. My parents realized how much discomfort I felt and eventually drove me to the family doctor an hour away. He pulled on the arm to get the should bone back in place and put me in a body cast that forced my arm to remain at chest level and wrapped my torso with a cast fully around my body. Later that week, Brother Wil had fun drawing a cartoon face on the front and the back of the head on the back of the cast.

Motivated by the desire to swim in an outdoor pool for a family vacation in Steamboat Springs, Colorado, I focused on wholeness and used my mind to heal in only four weeks. Maybe I wanted to get out of the cast and cartoon as fast as possible.

I clean up the flan with a paper towel and Miriam provides a fresh piece for me. I say, "I'm sorry, Miriam."

She says "You deserve a new one, maybe even more. I know you didn't mean to spill it. And thank you for cleaning it up. You are a very kind man."

After a delightful evening, Armando takes us to Hotel Yucatan. We thank him for his excellent driving and all that he did for us. I invite him to visit us if he ever comes to the states.

In the entrance to the hotel, we sing a *thank you* song that Violet has taught us. Sherry's children give him cards they made, adorned with shells they colored and found at the beach. Carlos and I give him an extra $50 each on behalf of all of us. "Adios," we say to our newfound friend. "¡Hasta luego!" (See you later).

Then we retire to our rooms; Sherry with her children, Quark with Carlos, and Violet and I together. She and I talk late into the night reminiscing about the perfect day and acknowledging our deep love as we merge in a full expression of spiritual, mental, emotional and physical love. I'm thinking, *"We are truly One!"*

Dr. Don Welsh

CHAPTER ELEVEN

The next morning is Sunday. Out of habit and a certain pull from Spirit; I had felt a desire the night before to hold a church service and had asked the front desk if there was a space we could use. We were shown to a small room with a table at the front and two dozen chairs, which they offered us, free of charge. Pleased with the set-up, we had then placed a hand-lettered flyer in the hotel lobby. Now, about a dozen tourists join the seven of us. I ask Carlos to lead the invocation.

He prays, "I am so touched by the Love-Energy of the Universe that blesses me with this opportunity to gather with my fellow travelers and these guests who have come together to celebrate the presence of Spirit in every moment.

I enter into a feeling of oneness with my fellow light-beings and speak my word for everyone here for this time together and for all we experience today. I am especially grateful that the Universal Wisdom shines through all of us, and that we are so blessed to be at this service. Many of us have had a meaningful journey to the heartland of the Mayas and I give thanks for the experiences.

I give thanks for Sherry and her children and that Yvette and Rev. Violet are always safe, and for my long time buddy, Dr. Donovan. We are so grateful for the richness that continues to uplift and embrace us. I bless everyone who came today. The Spirit of Love precedes each of us in our travels.

I release my word to the One Mind and the law of cause and effect reveals in the outer world of experience all the joy and gladness that I feel within. Knowing the Truth of these words, we claim it together saying, and So It Is…Y Asi Es!"

Violet echoes Carlos' closing, "So it is…Y asi es!" Then, she leads everyone in singing the *a capella* chant, "God's the Love that I Am."

The children learn it immediately. Their beautiful voices echo into the foyer. It is a moment I'll never forget.

I then guide a mostly silent meditation. I'm touched by the deep concentration Anton and Yvette show. They join me when I say, "And so it is."

I provide some insights for the day. "Whenever you forget the power you have within you, think of some examples that the many religions of the world have provided.

"Do you remember the wisdom of the Creation story? The Creative Process works like this: The seed of an idea is started by the masculine energy of the great vision. That vision is planted in the feminine mind that says 'yes' to the vision and sets about nurturing the idea to give it birth in the outer world. Always be grateful that this Creative Process is continuously manifesting the highest and greatest good for you.

"There are certain rules that the Universe follows as it cooperates with the Divine Good. Besides the commandments, why not recall the Ten Freedoms handed down by Moses. His people were supported using spiritual tools to bless all life.

Dr. Don Welsh

"Reading from the metaphysical interpretation of Exodus, by Donald Errol Welsh, God says, I am the Lord your God, who brought you out of the land of Egypt (sense communication) into freedom and these are ten of your freedoms:

1. You shall know that there is only one God; you shall not need to make anything else your God, neither worshipping nor serving them, since I show love to those who love me. You can use my name (or nature) for good.

2. You can keep a Sabbath Day holy. After you've been working hard, it feels good to relax. Labor for six days. Then take a day off using the original creation myth as your example.

3. You are to honor your parents, it feels good to share close family ties and the love for one another that is naturally there.

4. You are free to support life, keeping others alive. No one wants to destroy anyway.

5. You are free to be faithful enjoying mutual trust. You shall enjoy all of my abundance with no need to take from others.

6. You are free to be honest, always telling the truth.

7. You are free to know, with confidence, that there is plenty for everyone, in ample supply, because I am infinitely generous. There's just no need for the nagging feeling of jealousy.

8. Remember to honor the one Spirit at all times. Live by the law, knowing that what you put out comes back.

9. Remember the freedom you have to avoid taking from others. You are so richly rewarded, automatically. Remember the freedom you have when you honor alllife doing all you can to preserve it.

10. Forgive as you are forgiven. Humans make mistakes from time to time. Let go of blaming or placing shame on others. Thereby, you take guilt off yourself. Let your behavior toward others be such that you'd like to be treated that way yourself.

"That's enough for now. Thank you for your kind attention, especially you children. Live in the love that you are. I send blessings on your path."

To conclude our celebration, Rev. Violet gives a benediction or closing prayer:

"As we go forth, now, we set our intentions to experience life as best we possibly can. I give thanks for our spiritual experiences together, knowing we are so uplifted and blessed. Together, we say, and so it is!"

As people depart from the room, they thank us for an insightful and meaningful service. When the room is empty, Violet and I sit facing each other. Realizing our expenses have expanded beyond our original budget, we visualize money pouring out of an ATM machine.

I follow our visualization with a treatment (prayer).

"I know there is no lack or limitation in the universe. God is always providing ample supply. As Spiritual beings, Violet and I are prosperous. I see unlimited good coming to us continually and listen for divine ideas that turn into money! We are richly prospered in every moment and so grateful for it. And so it is!"

Violet joins me in the "and so it is" part.

The two of us leave the room exiting the hotel for a stroll in the pleasantly warm tropical evening.

Then, as we walk past a Banamex machine, money comes pouring out of the ATM!

Dr. Don Welsh

CHAPTER TWELVE

We silently express our thanks and scoop the money into Violet's purse for safe-keeping.

I say, "I've never heard of that happening before. I've known of computers getting confused and money being missing or added to people's accounts. And I've heard of slot machines malfunctioning."

"I once won on a slot machine" Violet says, "when the lights went out and all the slot machines where I was playing, started dropping silver dollars! But that was years ago, before the machines were perfected."

"It *is* several years ago in Mexico. Do you think we should contact the authorities?"

We looked for a phone booth because our cell phones had no signals.

"There's one," I say and when we walk up to the phone booth, I push an "O"

"Hola, policia."

"Hola. I'd like to report a broken ATM."

"Report it to the bank."

"Gracias."

"Adios."

I say to Violet, "We have to let the bank know."

"I'll look up the number in this phone book," she volunteers. She reads off the bank's number to me as I punch it in. I count how many times it rings; "Nineteen, twenty." Finally, a woman picks up.

I explain what has happened and she tells me to call the ATM company.

"Do you see a number for the ATM company?" I ask Violet.

"Uh. Oh, yes." She reads it off to me.

"Banamex, Buenas Dias."

"Do you speak English?"

"Si."

"My name is Donovan Wales and I just walked past an ATM machine that spilled out a bunch of money."

"Señor, our machines do not spill money out."

"This one did," I argue.

The woman replies indignantly, "I'm sorry; it must be some other bank. If you would like to report any other problems, please stay on the line."

I wait for her to come back, then repeat what happened. She again denies that their machines could spill out money and that if I want to report a crime, I should call the police.

I thank her, then, as I hang up, thank Spirit for the bountiful gift.

We look for a quiet restaurant to have a cup of Mexican coffee and maybe some desert as we walk along the busy street filled with vendors and early-evening shoppers.

A siren sounds in the distance. It gets closer and louder. Soon, it is right next to us, pulling up to the curb. Two officers get out of the squad car, and rush up.

"Buenas Noches, Señora y Señor. Are you the ones who took the money from the bank?"

"Yes. No. Well…" I stammer.

Dr. Don Welsh

"Which is it, yes or no?"

"No. Yes."

"Did you call the policia?"

"Yes. They told me to call the bank."

"It is good you did."

"But they told me to call Banamex and Banamex said to call the police."

"May I see your identification, Señor?"

I show him my passport. The shorter of the two watch us as the taller man goes to the cruiser and shines his light on my credentials.

When he comes back, he says, "Señor, this is not good. You will need to come with us back to the station."

"Oh, for crying out loud!"

"It's alright, Donovan. We can take a few minutes to help these gentlemen figure it out," Violet encourages.

"Regulations require that we have you put on these handcuffs."

I object. "What? This is not right. We just called you to clear all this up!"

"Donovan, it's okay…" Violet soothes.

I start raising my voice. Violet gently stops me, knowing how loud and intimidating my deep voice can be, even when I'm not angry.

But I *am* angry. I shut my mouth.

The police escort us into the back seat of the squad car. We head for headquarters with sirens blaring.

"This way," the desk sergeant instructs when we get there.

"You can explain it to the judge, later."

"How much later?" I ask.

Violet pokes me in the side. "Darr-leeng. It's okay!"

They put us in an interrogation room. We are left alone. Violet looks around, surveying the room for cameras. We don't see any. We wait. Apparently, no one hurries around here, because it is at least a half hour before anyone comes.

A thin, sprightly man with a clean shave, studies our documents and concludes, "So, I see you are *Americanos*."

"That's right."

"I am Luis Maderas. What is the purpose of your visit to Mexico? Is it business, Amigo?"

"Well, sort of. We're in the spiritual business. We're ministers. We're seeking Spiritual Gold."

"There, that's it. Spiritual Gold, you say?"

"Yes, through the Mayan ruins."

"That's on the report: *Spiritual Gold*."

"What report?"

"The one from the federales. Security heard you talking about it last week at the airport in Mexico City."

I almost blurt out, "Lopezs? Jorge Lopez?" but stop myself. Old anger buttons are starting to be activated, as I remember the guard at the airport in Mexico City when we first arrived.

Maderas continues, "The report mentions hostility. Is Spiritual Gold some new drug? A special meth formula, or marijuana?"

"No! Spiritual Gold."

"Oh!" The officer sneers. "Let me check my watch; is it 4:20? And do you want to smuggle it out of the country?"

Violet asks, "What's 4:20 refer to?"

"It's a slang reference to Cannabis Day," I explain.

Maderas makes notes and then asks Violet if she knows anything about Spiritual Gold.

"No," she says. "It's mainly Donovan's project."

"I thought so. Mrs. Wales, you will be allowed to go."

I point out, "Look. There wasn't really all that much money that came out of the Banamex. It looked like a lot. There was less than $100, but in pesos it just seemed like a lot more. I'll give it back."

The inspector says, "Oh, that's not what we're worried about. We're booking you for smuggling. You're either smuggling drugs or antiquities out of the country; Spiritual Gold."

"What proof do you have?"

"We'll figure it out over night."

I ask Violet to get a lawyer, a bail bondsman or maybe go to the American Embassy. She agrees as we say, goodnight with a clumsy embrace.

It is a noisy night in the Mexican jail. Privacy is out of the question. Sleep is even less likely.

Where's my friendly Maya Spirit NOW? I wonder.

I am given a bench for a bed, but at least it's mine. I get as comfortable as possible and focus on the Spirit within.

I ardently affirm, "There is one Power and Presence in the Universe and that Power is Divine Wisdom, Love and Goodness. God is everywhere present, including right here in this cell and right here within me. I claim protection for Violet as she is alone in the city and the hotel. I know she is

Divinely Guided in seeking assistance for me. I have a feeling of the Presence of All-Good.

"As a son of Spirit, my mind is One with the Universal Intelligence that goes right to the middle of this whole situation.

"I am free in Spirit and my Inner Divinity reveals anything I need to know or do to be released from this challenge. The Power that can do anything unlocks my cell and I am free to go and live fully right now."

I actually feel free already, so I continue, "An inner joy wells up in my heart and I am so grateful for my release. I am free!

"The Law of Cause and Effect does the rest and all is well. And so it truly is, right now!"

I meditate in that feeling. A couple of hours later, I realize I have slept. Then I hear the unlocking of the jail door.

It is barely light outside and I cry tears of joy as I see Violet and her beautiful face. Carlos and Quark are with her and they are prepared to pay the bail. But it isn't needed as the police realize they didn't have a case. Their smuggling conjectures were unfounded.

I feel badly for them and offer to give all the money back.

"Oh, no, Señor. We don't know anything about that. You have been put through a lot. We never saw any money! If you have any, keep it. You've earned it."

"I really want to do the right thing. Do you know anyone with the bank that I could talk to?

"Yes. Just a moment. I'll make a call." He leaves the room and returns in a few minutes with a smile on his face.

"I have good news, Señor Wales. The bank has no record of any money missing.

As we leave the police station and head for the hotel, about a dozen local children surround us offering *Chiclets* for a peso. Imagine their surprise when I hand each one the equivalent of one American dollar.

There is a chorus of gracias. "Gracias, Señora y Señor."

Carlos flags a taxi and we gratefully take it to the Yucatan Hotel. We wave at Sherry who has taken her children to the hotel pool.

As soon as we enter our room, I lie on the bed and immediately fall asleep with my clothes on.

After a few hours, I shower and Violet and I join Carlos and Quark for lunch and relate our recent happenings.

Carlos tells me, "You should have offered the police some of the money as a bribe."

"Carlos! I'm surprised at you," Violet teases.

"Well, *I'm* not the one who knew about Cannabis Day!"

CHAPTER THIRTEEN

The next morning, Quark knocks on our door. I answer in my pajamas.

"We must go to Miami." There is urgency in his voice.

"Why?"

"I have been sensing there is a special message there for you," says Quark.

"Just me?" I ask. "What about Violet?"

Quark says, "It really involves everyone."

"Well, what is it?"

"No one will understand unless they take the trip."

"Alright, I'll wake them up."

I suggest that we meet in about an hour, downstairs at the restaurant.

After we eat a quick breakfast and check out of the hotel, Carlos orders a taxi and we head for the Mexico City airport for a flight to Miami. Sherry wants to come with us, accompanied by her family. None of them have been there before.

Carlos questions the cost of all of them going, but Sherry says she has the money and will pay.

As we sit waiting for the flight to Miami, Carlos says, "I wouldn't want to pry, but where did you get that kind of money?"

"Well, you are prying. But that's okay. I don't mind if you and the Wales know."

Sherry includes Violet and me in her conversation. "Have you heard of Monte Carlo? The French Riviera?"

"Yes, of course," Carlos answers. "Why?"

Sherry says, "That is where my papa's family was from. At the end of World War II, there were many Russian officers in Germany. They had been given a lot of 'spoils of war' and were spending fortunes on gambling in Monte Carlo.

"My papa was a jeweler and the officers had an abundance of treasures they needed to sell. Papa gave them cash for gambling and stored the gold, silver, diamonds, pearls and other gems in a vault in his home on the French Riviera.

"He earned enough to move to the U.S. and started his own chain of jewelry stores. I was born in New Orleans. Eventually I married a Frenchman named Emile from Nice and I moved back there with him. Mama lived in the family home in New Orleans until two years ago. I spent the last three years of her life with her, taking care of her and helping her with financial matters.

"When she died, the house came to me.

"Emile, who was an officer in the French Foreign Legion was hospitalized from a wound he received in combat years before in Vietnam. He passed five years ago and his military insurance combined with Mama's money gave me a sizeable cushion so I don't have to work."

Your attention, please. The voice on the loudspeaker announced, *Flight 428, direct flight to Miami, Florida, is now boarding. All first class passengers and travelers with children are welcome to board now.*

Sherry and the children have first class tickets.

I ask Quark if he has his passport.

"What is a passport?" I show him mine. "Oh, I have no need of one of these. "I can go anywhere. On an airplane,

Dr. Don Welsh

I can sit anywhere. Remember, very few people can see me."

As Violet and I load, the "First Class" passengers are enjoying coffee and sweets. Quark has found an empty seat in the second row and seems to be enjoying himself thoroughly.

My body yearns for rest, and I fall into a relaxing sleep, awakened by the announcement, *We will be landing in Miami in ten minutes. Please make sure your seatbelt is fastened.*

It's a gentle landing. We collect our luggage and proceed to the Ground Transportation area. Next to the waiting area for rental cars, Quark notices a circular sign that says, "Pizza." He asks, "What is 'pizza?'"

"In a thousand years, you've never had pizza?" wonders Violet.

"No. Just enchiladas, tamales, chilies relleno, and even arroz con pollo, from Puerto Rico. But never pizza."

"*Prvention Magazine* had a recent article about pizza. It's supposed to be an almost perfect food with balanced nutrition," I comment.

As we step up to the pizza counter, Quark's jaw drops when he sees the "supreme" with pepperoni, ground beef and "the works." He lets us know he doesn't want meat.

I reassure him, "They have vegetarian pizzas and meatless calzones too."

He's a joy to watch as he tastes his first slice of pizza. He proclaims, "This is a spiritual experience!" We all laugh.

"Hmm. Pizzas are like people," he adds. "You see, each person is a circle with different pieces pointing to the center. That center is God and all the characteristics of Spirit come together in each piece to represent the Divine."

We marvel at his comparison. It reminds me of the simple explanations a teacher named Norman Vincent Peale wrote in his book, *The Power of Positive Thinking.*

Back in the 1950s, Peale had taught some of the New Thought ideas and brought them into the liberal Christianity of the day. Peale had piqued my interest. He studied the writings of Ernest Holmes and introduced them into his progressive Christian explanations. Recently, I've been prefacing my daily meditation by reading Peale. His wisdom is still current.

I studied many New Thought writers when I found the teaching now called Centers for Spiritual Living. I became a *Practitioner* (or prayer coach) when attending the San Jose Center. I went on to become a licensed minister while there. The in-depth course of study included counseling,

Dr. Don Welsh

psychology, writing, teaching, ethics, sermon preparation (homoletics), Bible interpretation and Church management.

It seems like it took a long time for me to 'get' that I was to be an ordained minister.

The final indicator was when I was released from my fulltime radio job. The boss called me into his office, handed me a severance check and told me they had sold the station to a broadcaster who planned to go "all Spanish." That was the very month (May) when I completed all my ministerial training, including an internship at the Santa Cruz Center for Spiritual Living, where Reverend Bob Jackson had agreed to be my mentor. He provided me with a lot of ministerial experiences including leading a Wednesday night service, teaching an advanced class on Thursdays to train *Practitioners,* and several opportunities to speak at Sunday services.

All those years studying and learning and here is a man named Quark who finds the key to God and the Universe in a pizza.

Noticing an ATM as we wait for our rental car, I anticipate a perfectly functioning machine as I step up to use it. Thankfully, the exact amount comes out; no more, no less.

Spiritual Gold - Mayan Mysteries for Our Modern Age

Dr. Don Welsh

CHAPTER FOURTEEN

Quark is curious.

As we settle into our rented van, Quark says, "Dr. Donovan, let me ask you something."

"Sure. What?"

"Whatever got you so interested in my people that you would go all the way to Mexico, explore our ruins and end up in a Mexican jail?"

I answered, "When I was declined from serving the Miami Center, I applied to the Ventura, California, Center and was impressed by the building. I read about it in order to understand why it drew me."

"Which was?" queries Quark.

Dr. Don Welsh

"The Mayan architecture," I reply. I find a postcard in my briefcase that shows a photo of the Ventura Center. "I had five thousand of these made. We used them for publicity. I brought a few with me to share with others we might meet on this trip."

Quark is impressed by the imposing magnificence of the Ventura structure. The 1933 building had been a strictly Western Hemispheric design rather than the usual Roman or Greek styles. It's now a subcategory of western architecture which the University of California at Santa Barbara claims as its own specialty.

Architect William Stacy-Judd, whose steps we followed in visiting the ruins, wrote about his explorations of Maya locations in the Yucatan Peninsula. He also made references to John Lloyd Stevens who had explored the Mayan ruins in the mid-1800s and described his discoveries in his journal, which included sketches by Frederick Catherwood, a 19th century British architect and sketch artist.

The current owners of the building are the members of the Ventura Center for Spiritual Living, who purchased the historic site from the First Baptist Church in 1958 when

Ernest Holmes, our movement's founder, was there to dedicate the building.

I became fascinated by the Maya and even organized a group excursion to the Yucatan Peninsula while ministering in Ventura.

A few years later, the Miami Center for Spiritual Living contacted me and invited me to re-apply for the Senior Minister position there. I accepted.

"And, what is significant about Miami?" Quark asked.

"The Everglades."

Carlos, who had been a member of the Miami Center, pointed out, "The funds from selling a twenty-year-old building enabled us to hire Dr. Donovan."

It was in Miami that I met Carlos. He served on the first ministerial selection committee I had encountered there. He was also my most trusted and loyal friend.

I tell Quark, "On Saturdays, I usually had opportunities to travel around the state and soak-in the warm climate. I loved Miami's North Beach, the Keys, especially Key West and other fun adventures all over the state."

My answer satisfies Quark, although he seems to know there were other reasons this area of Florida was important to me.

Dr. Don Welsh

As we travel south on the expressway, and pass a large hospital, it reminds me of one in Pomona, California, in the outskirts of L.A., about thirty miles east of downtown. I'd been working at K-WOW as the morning disc-jockey in Pomona.

My whole family had the flu. I was home in bed with it. My third daughter, Janey, was only seventeen months old at the time and it hit her hard. Later, when her condition worsened, my wife called the pediatrician's office.

Our regular doctor was out of town so we were told to rush Janey to the hospital. When my wife arrived, Janey began convulsing. It was evidently caused by dehydration. They gave her *Valium* and water to stop the convulsions, but she had an abnormal reaction to the drug and stopped breathing. The nurses were out of the room at the time, but fortunately my wife was there and immediately called for help. The staff rushed in, cleared the room and stabilized Janey. When my wife inquired about the prognosis, she spoke to the physician who had been called in for consultation. His name was Dr. Phillip Doubtful or Dr. Doubtful, for short.

True to his name, when asked if our baby would live, he said he didn't know. And if she did live, he didn't know how much brain damage might have occurred from lack of oxygen. My wife broke down and cried, but some other women in the visitor's room consoled her and she then called me to come to the hospital.

By that time, Janey was hooked up to intravenous liquids. The tubes entered one side of her head causing her to look disfigured. One side of her mouth also seemed to be drooping and she was unconscious.

After much angst, we realized there was nothing more for us to do but pray. We went to the local Unity Church. The kind secretary contacted the minister, who said she would pray from her home, and we sat in the sanctuary in meditation and prayed for about two hours.

When we anxiously returned to the hospital, Janey was wide-awake, the tubes had been removed, her face was normal and she said, "Daddy!" I hugged and kissed her and cried, while thanking God for the miracle.

Janey has never suffered any ill effects from the incident. (She does have a quirky personality, however.)

Mayan Spiritual Insight Number Nine: *Prayer works.*

Quark points out the healer doesn't need to be present for the patient to be restored to Wholeness.

I return to my answer of why the Everglades are so special to me. "I feel as if a significant spiritual event for me is going to happen here. Back in the 1990's, I read the best selling book, *The Celestine Prophecy*. In it, James Redfield outlined nine 'Insights,' which were supposed manuscripts from ancient Peruvians.

"Redfield followed up with *The Tenth Insight* where the participants journeyed to beautiful places in nature. They visited rainforests, mountains and other vortexes where they could tune in to the highest insights for their lives."

Anton asks, "What's a vortex?"

I explain, "A vortex is an energy pocket that electrical engineers can pinpoint and measure."

Yvette says, "You mean like a pocket in my dress?'

Violet smiles and says, "Very clever, sweetie. "I suppose you're right, if your dress had the ability to have an electrical charge."

Carlos adds, "A vortex is kind of like the feeling you get on a merry-go-round."

Anton asks, "Dr. Donovan, were you ever in a vortex?"

"Well, yes. But there are two kinds; one is a feminine vortex, in which you feel the energy coming down into a gully and a masculine vortex, where you feel uplifted in an upward swoop of energy."

"That's cool," says Anton.

I continue, "I learned about vortexes while hiking in Sedona, Arizona, years ago. After reading Redfield's books, I determined that such a quest would be useful to my ministry, but where would I find a rainforest in the flatland swamps of Florida?"

"Right here in the swamp lands," Carlos observes.

"Exactly," I say, "the Everglades National Park, just south of here, is classified as a rain forest. Most of it is shallow water that looks like a lake. But there are small islands of old-growth trees which drip acidic tree sap into the water and onto the coral lake bottom, which carves out borders to the hammocks.

"We decide to drive south to the Park and walk along the path made of boards, where I found a thousand year old mahogany tree.

Carlo's says, "Quark's age"

Everyone snickers, but Quark doesn't respond.

Violet says, "I'll bet you hugged that old tree."

"As a matter of fact, I did."

"Let's go see it!" Violet says enthusiastically.

"Unfortunately, I heard it was destroyed by a hurricane a few years ago."

"Why is it so important to you?" she asks.

"I sense the tree has guidance for me and my ministry.

We walk along a boardwalk path until we come to a big hole in the jungle where the trunk of the tree once was. A marker says that the tree had been destroyed on April 29, 2005 by hurricane Katrina. In a silent moment, I feel a sadness, as if a good friend had departed.

I find a nearby bench and Violet and I sit there. I suggest that everyone find seats and we'll all vision again, like we did in the van. But this time, there are no distractions because it's quieter and there are no other vans, cars or trucks to avoid. I go through the process of telling everyone to relax and focus their attention upwardly and inwardly to listen for the highest idea in the mind of God for whatever they want guidance about.

For myself, I ask, "What is the highest idea in the mind of Spirit for my ministry? The answer comes, loud and clear. Spirit says, 'WRITE!'"

"*No,*" I object, "My brother, Wil, is The Writer in the family. I'm 'The *Voice*' (after all, I was a DJ at one time).

"So, I asked Spirit again. I hear, 'You're a WRITER'."

Sure, I have written copy for broadcast commercials and as a minister, have written newsletters and sermons, but my older brother, Wil Wales, has written books, magazine articles, television scripts, plays, and novels.

I insist, "No, God, my brother's 'The Writer.'"

Then it hit me. I'm a writer and if I wrote books based on the Spiritual ideas we teach, it would enhance and uplift our ministry.

"Now, I realize that writing is my Spiritual Gold. Finally, I listened and now intend doing Spirit's work more fully. It gives me gratification and purpose. My life experiences have been synchronized and have generated personal fulfillment and abundance." I share my vision with Violet and the others. Violet says, "I was told that Dr. Donovan and I should write a column in the newspaper!"

Quark says, "I believe Spirit has Its own message for everyone. If there is something God wants to whisper to someone, they better be listening."

"And visioning is one way we can listen." I say.

Dr. Don Welsh

Quark continues, "And what message do other people have for you? Everyone is a messenger. The Maya have a message for you. Be still and hear the divine ideas. And then, follow what you're told. You, too, are meant to prosper and live in fulfillment."

Carlos and Sherry sit on a nearby bench and when it is time to share their visions, Carlos says, "I got the message to…marry…marry…Sherry!"

Sherry is surprised and reacts with a sudden eye opening "What? Me, too! I'm supposed to marry you, Carlos. Oh! My God!"

Violet says, "I knew it! When?"

Carlos explains, "I didn't know it until just now. And I can hardly believe it. I'm so grateful I found Sherry."

Sherry gloats, "He's more than I could have ever imagine: loving, kind, considerate, and he likes children."

They glow as Yvette and Anton chorus, "We finally have a dad!"

"Now, the only concern is what people will think about such a whirlwind courtship," says Sherry.

Carlos kids, "My only concern is, where can we find a minister to perform the ceremony?"

Violet says, "Do you want one of us or two?"

Sherry answers, "Two"

"And when?"

"April 29th. The day Katrina destroyed the mahogany tree." says Sherry.

"It's October now," says Violet. "Will that give you enough time?"

Yvette says, "I can help!"

Anton says, "Me, too."

Dr. Don Welsh

CHAPTER FIFTEEN

Everyone seems to have accomplished their goals. Violet and I have received the vision to write, Sherry and Carlos have found each other, the children are getting a new dad. Quark is enjoying teaching us.

I dread a stop in Mexico City because of my previous experiences with Sarjente Lopez. Carlos drives every one back to the Miami airport and we decide to join up the next day in Guatamala by way of Mexico City. It is the gateway to Central America, and Quark wants us to see Tikal in Guatamala before concluding our explorations.

In the movie *The Secret*, we learned to focus on what we

Dr. Don Welsh

do want, not what we *don't* want.

My expectations are realized when our plane lands in Mexico City. I get what I don't want! Once again, we are surrounded by flashing lights and blaring sirens. Apparently, the authorities notified the Mexico City airport that their "dangerous fugitive" was arriving.

The flight attendant opens the door and two armed guards come aboard. There he is, Jorge Lopez, rifle in hand.

"Mr. Donovan Wales. Mr. Wales, step forward with your arms raised!"

I do as I'm told. I walk up the aisle with my arms up, greet my least favorite airport policeman, Jorge Lopez, and say: "Hola."

"Hola, Gringo," he says with his rifle pointed directly at my heart. "We're going to *La oficine de Costumbres Nationale* Customs."

When we have made our way through the confusion, the gaping tourists and the long walk to his office, I am ordered to be seated and Lopez asks me, "I heard they had you in custody. Did you escape, Mr. Wales? And where's the stuff…the loot…the antiquities?"

"Doctor."

"Qué?"

"Doctor Wales. Dr. Donovan Wales. That's why I've been searching for Spiritual Gold. It's a metaphor, not literal gold, but something people value even more than money. It's like Jesus told the woman at Jacob's Well, 'I can give you living waters.'"

Suddenly, I feel the need to back off and simply let Lopez remain in the dark. I can't seem to convince him of my innocence. Naively, I figure, as long as I haven't done anything wrong, I can't be arrested, anyway.

Suddenly, Lopez seems to quiver and shake. He lowers his rifle. "What did you just do, Wales?"

"Nothing, why? I just decided to let go of my argument of innocence. I'm just telling the truth, anyway."

"The truth, so help you, God?"

"That's right," I assure him.

"So your Spiritual Gold is just knowing the Truth and you get rewarded for it, sort of?"

"Right. Rewarded for following Divine guidance just doing what God wants."

Jorge thrusts his hand forward to shake mine. "Does God want you to board your next airplane, now?"

"Yes, to Tikal."

Dr. Don Welsh

"Well then, you'd better go. That airplane leaves in ten minutes. Safe travels."

And with that, Lopez surprises me with a heartfelt hug. I feel so open and free. The prior anger completely disappears.

Sarjente Lopez provides an officer with a cart to rush us to the gate and we wave to Jorge as we board the plane to Goldson International in Tikal.

With what seems like a celebrity sendoff, we get on the plane, find our seats and smoothly ascend.

This is a smaller plane than the one we took from Merida to Miami and there is no separate First Class area. I sit in a three seat section. Violet is next to the window and Yvette is on the aisle. She asks me, "Mr. Doctor Donovan, do you ever get angry?"

"Yes. Do you? "

"Only with my brother. He teases me sometimes and I don't know why I let that bother me."

"Who? Anton?"

"Qui. I know he really likes me, but he teases me because I'm a girl."

"I have an older brother, too."

"Does he tease you?

"Yeah. Always has, ever since we were kids."

"What about?"

"I think he sensed I thought there was something wrong with me and he took advantage of that. Since my parents used the phrase "¿Qué pasa con tigo?" which I thought meant "What's the matter with you?" I thought they were right and that there really was something wrong with me. They said the same thing to my brother, but since he was older, he understood the phrase differently and wasn't bothered by it. Now, I understand that it means "What's going on?"

"But when my brother says I'm stupid because I'm a girl, it must be true because I am a girl."

"Yes, but there have been some very smart girls!"

"Really? Who?" Yvette wonders.

There was Madame Curie. She and her husband discovered radium. And she was the smart one of the team.

We land at Philip Goldson International Airport and board a shuttle bus which takes Quark, Sherry, Carlos, Yvette, Anton, Violet and me directly to the ruins at Tikal, Guatemala.

To me, these ruins are even more dramatic than all the others. We stand in the Plaza of the Seven Temples. Quark points out that seven is a mystical number representing completion.

Carlos says, "With my soon-to-be new family, I'll be complete. But, I have just one question, Quark. You were alive when these fantastic pyramids were built, right?"

"That is correct. What is your question?"

"Well then, how, did the ancient Maya build them? The pyramids, I mean?"

We all gather close to Quark as he says quietly, "Let me explain. According to what you call *Newton's Law of Gravity*, every object in the universe attracts every other object. The gravitational force had to be overcome in order to lift the huge stones. They needed to invoke levitation.

"There are two ways to understand levitation: mathematically and spiritually."

I ask, "Carlos, can you translate that?"

"Oh, yeah. Newton was a physicist, first. He came up with a lot of ways to understand the universe, but before that, the Maya discovered levitation."

Anton asks, "Do you mean people floated?"

"Quark answers, "Yes, and better than that, they had spiritual understanding.

"I want that," says Yvette.

Violet comments, "You already have it. I saw your spirit in the cave. You were a brave girl. You know God is always protecting you."

Quark continues, "Furthermore, there is an inverse force, attracting the objects away from the other. This is an anti-gravity power. It causes a pushing and a pulling at the same time. The result is a tremendous force much like the Love Energy of the Universe, or the Power for Good, being heightened."

He adds, "When releasing a sense of ego and self-absorption, one may find levitation possible through a reinforcement loop which develops. As one believes in the possibility of levitation, that loop grows even stronger."

Anton says, "I believe I can levitate, therefore, I can?"

Quark smiles. "Whenever you notice a sense of doubt, switch to a positive attitude and know that your good is increasing, exponentially. It is similar to a snowball rolling downhill, picking up volume as it rolls. There is a power in like energy."

I say, "That's the same energy that keeps you healthy."

"And youthful" Violet affirms.

I give her a wink, then add, "What I've come to learn is how powerfully people can use their minds to focus the energy and actually mold their lives – everything from prosperity and success to creativity and love relationships".

Quark says, "It's similar to the hidden pyramids under hills of dirt."

"Yeah," notes Carlos, "Everywhere around here, in other parts of Guatemala, in Belize and throughout Mexico, if you notice a hill with a shape similar to a pyramid, chances are, it is one. It took a lot of digging for archeologists to uncover these ruins, but underneath it all, they found Spiritual Gold."

Quark looks as if he's ready to leave as magically as he appeared. His vast wisdom and giving qualities have advanced people for generations. We each have been profoundly altered by his presence.

As Quark departs, he promises to make himself available whenever any of us need spiritual support. "I'll bring my thousand years of wisdom to you wherever you are, or to whomever needs it. That is my new mission. I've decided to live in the spiritual dimension to give me easier availability to all who ask. So, don't forget, your Friendly Maya Spirit is always with you."

He starts to go, then turns back saying, "One more thing, 'qué pasa' is a friendly greeting."

"I know, Carlos already told me. I realize what a strong affect that misunderstanding had on me. It has changed my entire life. The adult living as me is more than aware that my parents' innocent usage of that phrase carried over to a major attitude. I promise I won't let it bother me ever again. That is my Spiritual Gold. I'm going to have to revise how I've interpreted my life. In fact, my attitude adjustment has already begun."

"Good for you."

Before we lost him to the ether, we say to one another and to Quark, "¡Qué pasa, Amigos!"

Then, we all feel the warmth of an unforgettable group hug.

The End

Dr. Don Welsh

THE NINE MAYA SPIRITUAL INSIGHTS

Number One: *God is neither masculine nor feminine, but both.*

Number Two: *There is only one God of movement and motion.*

Number Three: *Sometimes losing is winning; sometimes winning is losing.*

Number Four: *Since we are one with God, we are immortal beings.*

Number Five: *All beings are made of Love.*

Number Six: *As a Spiritual being, you can use your spiritual talents to transform your life and the lives of others.*

Number Seven: *Humans recreate the process by which God creates the universe.*

Number Eight: *For God's vision regarding an area of your life, vision for ideas about the highest good.*

Number Nine: *Prayer works.*

Dr. Don Welsh

ABOUT THE AUTHOR

Dr. Don Welsh spent 23 years in broadcasting as an announcer and personality DJ. He studied Unity and Science of Mind (now Centers for Spiritual Living) teachings as early as 1968 and began his ministry in Ventura, California in 1989, moving to Miami, Florida; Lancaster, California and together with Rev. LaVonne, the Central Coast Center for Spiritual Living in Templeton, California, beginning in 2009.

In the mid-1990s, he received a vision from Spirit to take up writing. It took him until 2014 to publish his first book, *The Mystical 10*, immediately followed by *New Thought Genesis*, *New Thought Exodus* and with Rev. LaVonne, *Divine Dialogues*.

Spiritual Gold, Mayan Mysteries for Our Modern Age is his first spiritual fiction book.

Dr. Don Welsh may be contacted at
The Central Coast Center for Spiritual Living,
689 Crocker St., Templeton, CA 93465
(661) 433-7383
www.cccenterforspiritualliving.org
donwelsh@sbcglobal.net
revlavonne@sbcglobal.net

Dr. Don Welsh

Spiritual Gold - Mayan Mysteries for Our Modern Age

Dr. Don Welsh

www.ingramcontent.com/pod-product-compliance
Lightning Source LLC
Chambersburg PA
CBHW022117040426
42450CB00006B/734